(Cover) *'Pipit,' one of the most popular daffodils in culture today, is wonderfully fragrant.*
(Page 1) *Levi the cat daydreams while smelling the 'Jumblie' daffodils.*
(Pages 2-3) *N. 'Arctic Gold,' a long-lasting, all yellow, blue ribbon winning, classic trumpet daffodil, has smooth petals and lots of substance.*
(Pages 4-5) *'Accent,' with its pink cup, shows up well against the green foliage of campanula.*
(Pages 6-7) *An all-white garden features the daffodil 'Stainless,'* Leucojum aestivum, Muscari *'Argaei Album',* and Anemone blanda *'White Splendour.'*

Daffodils

FOR NORTH AMERICAN GARDENS

BY BRENT AND BECKY HEATH

bright sky press

albany, texas • new york, new york

bright sky press
Albany, Texas · New York, New York

Library of Congress Cataloging-in-Publication Data

Heath, Brent, 1945-
    Daffodils for North American gardens / by Brent and Becky Heath
        p.cm.
    Rev. ed. of: Daffodils for American gardens. c 1995
    Includes bibliographical references (p.).
    ISBN 0-9704729-7-8 (alk. paper)
        1. Daffodils — United States. 2. Daffodils — Canada. 3. Daffodils.
I. Heath, Becky, 1945- II.Heath, Brent, 1945-
Daffodils for American gardens. III. Title.

    SB413.D12 H43 2001
    635.9'3434'097 — dc21

                        2001043146

Book and Cover Design: Gibson Parsons Design
Edited by Diane Furtney

Revised edition designed by Anne Masters Design, Inc.
Photography by Brent Heath
Editorial Direction, revised edition: Vivienne Jaffe
Distributed by: Sterling Publishing Co., Inc.
Printed in China through Asia Pacific Offset

Contents

Preface

BRENT'S PREFACE

I've spent the better part of my 56 years being involved with the genus *Narcissus (N.)*, commonly known as daffodils. I grew up on a daffodil farm in Gloucester County (Tidewater) Virginia, where my parents, Katharine and George Heath, owned and operated the Daffodil Mart. In my childhood the Mart amounted to a group of minifarms (about ten 5– to 10–acre plots) where bulbs were grown for mail-order business and flowers were picked and shipped to wholesale florists and individual customers. At one time my parents listed more than 1,500 cultivars and varieties of daffodils in their catalog.

The daffodil industry in Virginia, including my family's early involvement, centered around my grandfather, Charles Heath, who moved to the area in 1900. He established a bulb business based on a cottage industry of harvesting the *N. pseudonarcissus* ("Early Virginia," "Lent Lily," and "Trumpet Major") that grew so abundantly here. An article about him, "Gold Was Where He Found It," appeared in *Reader's Digest* in March 1956. It's a delightful story of how my grandfather

(Pages 8-9) *The graceful, pendulous blossoms of N. 'Tuesday's Child' stand out beautifully against the darker T. 'Orange Emperor'.* (Below) *A patch of 'Early Virginia' has persisted at Dunham Massie, a farm in Gloucester County, Virginia, for at least a hundred years.*

began importing newer and better cultivars, then growing and selling them to local farmers. The farmers in turn found a ready market during the Depression years when the daffodil was considered the "Poor Man's Rose." My grandfather's industry prospered, with hundreds of local families devoting anywhere from one-quarter acre to several hundred acres to flower production inspired by Charles Heath.

Matthew Zandbergen finds his "pot of gold" in the form of wild golden daffodils under a rainbow in the Pyrenees.

Because of this flower boom, Van Wavern, a Dutch firm, was attracted to this area. Van Wavern based its American operations here when there was an embargo on Dutch bulbs between the First and Second World wars. The Van Wavern operation, estimated to have had between 500 and 600 acres in bulb production here, employed several hundred local people. My father, George Heath, managed this operation until the Second World War when Van Wavern returned to Holland.

I grew up on the Daffodil Mart farm. I recall tagging along and helping out in various ways. My parents encouraged my participation and even gave me a start at growing my own bulbs on a small piece of land nearby. They let me gather the smallest offsets, or "chips," from the bulb grader for me to plant on my plot.

My first daffodils took several years to mature. But each year I'd harvest more flowers that my friends and I would sell locally to tourists and visitors, The bonanza came when I was about nine: when I dug my first crop, I had about 20 bushels of saleable bulbs for which my parents paid me five dollars per bushel. I was a rich man that summer. I bought myself a used skiff and a new bike. My friends were envious and most of them came to work at the Daffodil Mart at one time or another, too. But digging bulbs is hot, hard, dirty work, and not many of them came back after one season.

The childhood enterprise that had been like a fairy tale for me began to fade when I was old enough to be paid to work by the hour. The grimy job of digging bulbs for my parents in the hot summer sun just didn't feel the same as digging my own. I worked much harder baling hay for a farmer friend. But through my teenage years I remained interested in botany and natural history. One summer I started work at Nature Camp, a nature-study camp for children, as a counselor and teacher. I continued to help at home with the family business while I went to college.

The family enterprise had gradually changed due to my father's illness. Using a trial farm of ten acres, my mother then built one of the loveliest daffodil display gardens in the country. Several hundred cultivars were shown in sweeps of 50 to 100 of each variety. Between the middle of March and the end of April each year, we'd get as many as 20,000 visitors. Articles about the display garden were featured in many major newspapers and magazines all over the country.

When my mother became ill, I left college to run the business while she recovered. Then in 1972, after a stint of four years as director of Nature Camp, I began to buy the Daffodil Mart from my mother. With her help and help from my parents' friends and associates, I began to expand the farm. I'd like to acknowledge gratefully that Matthew Zandbergen purchased new equipment in Holland for me and introduced me to the more progressive growers there. Grant Mitsch generously shared his bulbs and his knowledge, once writing 25 typed pages for me about all aspects of cultural procedures in the industry; on another occasion he sent me a long paper on hybridizing.

Murray Evans also shared his bulbs and his expertise. It was Murray who helped me find equipment and become familiar with the West Coast bulb industry. Frederick Baukages set up my Heath Enterprises Corporation and provided financial advice. Bill and Laura Lee Ticknor have been loyal and supportive friends through the ups and downs of business over the years. And it was Kathy Andersen who finally convinced me that being a daffodil judge would be an enjoyable way to share my interest and knowledge.

Katie Heath, Brent's mother, enjoys the fragrance and beauty of some of our seedlings.

At one point during the 1970s, when our farm was located in the adjacent county of Mathews, we had almost 100 acres under daffodil bulb production. But in the late 1970s I moved the farm back to Gloucester, greatly reduced the acreage by transferring some cultivars to Dutch growers in Holland, and sold bulk quantities of bulbs to growers in Washington state. At about that same time I married Becky and, combining our families of four children, took up the project of breeding daffodils. Since then our business has grown from a two-adult outfit, with Becky driving the tractor and the children and I riding the bulb digger, to a multinational business handling millions of bulbs.

At present, we sell bulbs to both wholesalers and retail purchasers. We have a business and warehouse here in Virginia with about 30 part-time and a few full-time employees. We have a business and another warehouse in Holland, managed by John de Goede, and a network of more than 100 growers who produce the majority of our bulbs under contract and special agreements. We work closely with growers in Virginia and North Carolina who provide several cultivars for us. We also import some bulbs from growers in England and Israel.

Our company, Brent and Becky's Bulbs, works closely with a number of public gardens and universities (see "Daffodil Gardens on Display"), where trial gardens and research projects related to daffodils are ongoing. We've established another extensive trial and display garden here on our 10-acre farm in Gloucester, where thousands of cultivars of bulbs are planted in every way imaginable to offer ideas to gardeners about how to use bulbs effectively. Our garden is open in the spring, by appointment, for guided tours and throughout the year for seminars and workshops. Feel free to contact us about our annual tour schedule. Check our website www.brent andbeckysbulbs.com for schedule.

In recent years I've begun a lecture series on daffodils and other bulb plants. This is taking me all over the country to a broad variety of audiences. In 2000 alone I conducted workshops and presentations in 45 different cities.

Becky still drives a tractor sometimes, but she has also put

This view of the trial field at Brent and Becky's Bulbs was taken from our bedroom window.

together a computer system to keep our business running smoothly. This has been quite a feat sometimes, keeping up with annual growth. I am a dreamer and the idea person; she is the realist who makes it all work. Our mutual vision is to help others see the brightest side of the world we live in, through gardening. The therapy of gardening gladdens our hearts, gives us a sense of peace and harmony with the world we are a part of but so often feel apart from. Flowers are good for people; flowers make people cheerful. Sometimes we look upon our planting efforts as being in the business of planting smiles.

BECKY'S PREFACE

I was raised in an affectionate, disciplined, traditional family in which my Dad went to work while Mom stayed home to care for the three children. We eventually became a family with two working parents, but we still spent lots of time together and always had a big vegetable garden where we all helped. For a while we also had pigs, geese, and rabbits. My great-uncle was a farmer with impressive tractors and combines, and I really enjoyed visiting him and helping as much as I could around his farm.

Growing flowers, however, was not a priority for our family. The neighborhood children played in our yard, and the bare spot in the grass that constant baseball and football games created was just fine with my parents because, to their way of thinking, it was better to keep a close watch on their children than to have a perfect lawn or a flower garden on display.

I grew up, went to college (where I majored in music education), and ventured into adult life by teaching music in public schools and directing church choirs. I continued to plant a vegetable garden. By the time I met Brent, I also had pigs, chickens, two wonderful sons, and a productive vegetable patch, but not many flowers. I was still living by the maxim, "If you can't eat it, don't grow it!"

I typed a catalog for Brent in 1979. All the catalog contained was an alphabetical listing of about 400 daffodils with a strange code consisting of numbers, letters, and symbols after each flower name. I asked him how people could figure out what to order just from looking at that list. He replied that his customers were educated about daffodils and knew what they wanted; they really only needed the flower name and price. I told him I might want to buy flowers from him, but there was no way I'd know what to order since the catalog didn't even have an explanation of the codes. I think that was when our relationship began to bloom!

I began to absorb information about bulb plants as I worked more with Brent. I think when a person grows up with a subject the way Brent did, he assumes that everyone else shares a lot of his knowledge. But I knew I wasn't the only person who didn't know a thing about daffodil bulbs. As I learned more, that information filtered into our catalog and into our planting instructions.

Brent and Becky Heath

In 1984, I bought Brent his first pocket-sized tape recorder so that he could begin recording information while driving. Often, though, he'd forget to turn it on, so I bought him a voice-activated recorder. I guess one could say that I had been pushing for us to put this book together for about 10 years.

And here is our *Daffodils*, revised and updated. It summarizes much of what we've discovered across the years about the wide subject of daffodils. We hope the book will help all your gardening efforts and bring you, your family, and your neighbors a great deal of enjoyment.

I. Introduction to Daffodils

NAMES: DAFFODILS, *NARCISSUS*, JONQUILS

The word "daffodil" brings to mind those bright yellow blossoms that begin to appear as if by magic, that help to end the winter doldrums and bring early life to the spring garden. We don't all refer to them by the same name, however, and sometimes the terms have been confused.

Narcissus is the formal Latin or botanical term for the whole genus of these bulbous plants of the Amaryllis family. Over the years people have mistakenly referred to certain types of these plants as "narcissus" (usually the tazetta types having clusters of flowers), while thinking that other varieties were "daffodils." Actually, daffodil and *Narcissus* are interchangeable since daffodil is the common or English name for all members of the genus *Narcissus*.

There are a few other terms for daffodils that are misused. In the southeastern part of the States, "jonquil" is often used for daffodil because early colonists from England brought with them jonquilla-type bulbs. When these were planted in the new country their blooms were called "jonquils," which is exactly what they were.

This sweetly fragrant little bulb, which makes up the seventh division in the thirteen divisions of daffodils, found the southeastern states so much like its native home that jonquils became naturalized over a fairly wide area. They had grown this way for a couple of centuries before modern hybrid daffodils became widely available. As time passed and the larger trumpet types of daffodils came across the ocean, many people erroneously called them jonquils too, or "johnny-quils." So when your southern cousins speak fondly of their jonquils, you'll know that they're talking about daffodils.

If your midwest or southern relations mention their "buttercups," they are usually referring to what's known as "daffy-down-dillies." All you really need to remember is that these wonderful flowers are correctly called either daffodils or *Narcissus* regardless of the floral division in which they fall.

The word "Narcissus," by the way, has an interesting origin in addition to the familiar legend of the handsome Greek lad who admired his reflection in a pool, fell in, drowned, and

(Pages 16-17) *The daffodil 'Carbineer,' a N. 'Pinza' look-alike, shares its bed with candytuft, basket-of-gold, flowering quince, and Mahonia. The combination shows off the daffodils to their best advantage.* (Opposite) *'Birma' is equally close to perfection on the show bench or in the garden.* (Above) *'Redhill' is a sunproof daffodil with substance so thick that it lasts for a long time.*

was changed into a nodding flower reflected in the water. The derivation of the word has to do with the "narcotic" and poisonous alkaloid found in the bulbs. When ingested, this alkaloid produces a quick stupor and death. It has been said that Roman warriors carried *Narcissus* bulbs in their saddle bags; when mortally wounded, the soldier would eat one and dreamily pass off into the land of the gods.

It would have taken a strong-willed individual to eat one, however, because the alkaloid crystals are extremely distasteful and create great discomfort in the mouth. As a rule you do not have to worry about a child being accidently poisoned from eating daffodil bulbs. We have heard of someone mistaking the bulbs for onions, but quickly realizing the error from the unpleasant sharp taste. The juice or sap from the stem can also be an irritant to the skin, but most people are not affected by it at all.

The poisonous character of *Narcissus* does give the gardener a real advantage. The alkaloid fluid acts as a strong repellant to most pests; indeed, the daffodil has few insect predators (see "Insects and Diseases"). The alkaloid is also being researched and developed by several pharmaceutical companies as a possible drug component in the treatment of Alzheimer's and several other diseases.

The alkaloid is not addictive, but daffodils can be. This is such a carefree, pest-free, drought-tolerant, diverse, and beautiful group of plants that you can easily fall prey to their narcotic appeal and get hooked on them!

DAFFODIL SPECIES AND WILD FORMS

Bulbs of the genus *Narcissus* occur in the wild in southwestern Europe in a relatively small range that stretches from Spain and Portugal up to France and Great Britain, over to Switzerland and Austria, then back down to Greece and Italy. A few wild species grow in North Africa.

The graceful and fragrant Narcissus jonquilla *is native to southern France and Spain. The* Narcissus *species brought by the early colonists to southeastern North America, where it happily naturalized, was the* jonquilla. *This is why many southerners today call big, hybrid daffodils "jonquils." (Below)* N. poeticus *var.* recurvas *is native to Austria and naturalizes best in cool climates.*

There are between 50 to 100 species *Narcissus* (wild daffodils) in addition to a fair number of subspecies (variations of species) and wild hybrids. Unfortunately their names tend to change at the whim of botanists. Jokingly, we say that botanists maintain their job security by periodically changing the species' names. Changes happen so often that it can be a bit discouraging to a gardener who has just managed to learn a new botanical term.

However, Michael Salmon and John Blanchard, both Englishmen, are continuing projects to document species in their native habitats with the intent of systematically identifying and classifying them. John Blanchard's book, *Narcissus —A Guide to Wild Daffodils*, is an excellent resource for anyone interested in learning more about these beautiful little plants.

Michael Salmon, whose life's work and business have been with species bulbs, is now finishing up the most complete document on species *Narcissus*. His art work depicting each of these charming flowers is meticulously accurate. His microscopic method of identification according to the arrangement of vascular bundles (the xylem and phloem tubes) in the leaves is the most reliable system of identification to date.

The Austrian Alps are home to the wild N. poeticus var. recurvus ("Pheasant's-Eye").

More research has been done by Kathy Andersen from Delaware, a past president of the American Daffodil Society, who has spent several spring seasons traveling and documenting species in Europe. A series of articles on her travels and discoveries has been published in The American Daffodil Society's *Daffodil Journal*.

Wild daffodil species suffer in many areas from encroachment as human populations increase and people begin to develop or farm where native plant populations exist. Also there has been a good deal of controversy about the collection and sale of wild plants and bulbs. Any species *Narcissus* should be purchased from a supplier who states that the bulbs are nursery-propagated and not wild-collected.

Species bulbs tend to be expensive because they are hard

to come by and not easy to propagate. If you find species bulbs offered at a low price, they have probably been wild-collected or are misnamed. "Buyer beware" is a good idea if a deal sounds too good to be true or if fancy unregistered names are used to describe the species bulbs.

Before you purchase species bulbs, please read up on their cultural requirements in a book such as John Blanchard's *Narcissus*. Then find or create that special area on your property where you think these little flowers will have a chance to thrive and multiply. Once you have them growing well, help Mother Nature along by pollinating the flowers (see "Naturalizing"). Harvest and plant the seeds and share them with other gardeners. The larger species bulbs often behave a lot like larger established hybrid plants. They tend not to be as specific in their requirements or as much of a challenge to grow as some other, fussier daffodils.

THE DAFFODIL INDUSTRY, PAST AND PRESENT

Narcissus tazetta bulbs, whose origin is in European countries bordering the Mediterranean, have been found in China and other Asian countries for many hundreds of years. The daffodil bulb industry probably dates back to the earliest days of trading between the West and East.

In England and other parts of Europe, wild daffodils were gathered by early botanists searching for medicinal uses of wild plants. Later on, daffodils were recognized for their ornamental attributes, and gardeners began to cross-pollinate to create new hybrids.

Literature as far back as *Gerard's Herbal* (published 1545–1612) mentions daffodils and their uses. A few of the earliest hybrids and most of the species mentioned by Peter Barr in *Ye Narcissus or Daffodyl Flowre, and hys Roots* (1884) are still available today.

Great Britain has always led the world in the creation of hybrids and in the overall production of *Narcissus* bulbs. The majority of the more than 25,000 daffodil cultivars have been developed in the British Isles. Both England and Ireland are well-known for excellent daffodil hybridizing.

Kate Reed, with help from her grandson and Becky, select near-perfect flowers for a show in Northern Ireland.

The bulk of bulb production stays located in Cornwall, Lincolnshire, Norfolk, and the Scilly Isles. Several British cooperatives handle wholesale sales to the United States. Many of the bulbs you find in garden centers, discount outlets, and other mass markets are English bulbs. A number of those have been marketed through Dutch distribution channels for both mail-order and garden-center sales.

English bulbs tend to be a bit smaller and more solid than their Dutch counterparts. They are generally of good quality, depending on the grower. Sometimes the bulbs are misnamed or have rogues. The bulbs are suitable for mass planting but not specific display.

While the Dutch have been associated with the word "bulb" since the 17th century, and now produce a vast quantity of the world's bulb crop, The Netherlands is still second in the production of daffodils. While English and Irish breeders have been more concerned with producing flowers for exhibition, Dutch breeders have focused on hybridizing daffodils for forcing, for cut flowers, and for home gardens.

A new division of interesting and unusual split-corona and sunburst daffodils have come from Dutch hybridizing. The quality of daffodil bulbs coming from Holland now is superb. Overall, the level of horticulture in Holland is far above what we have seen anywhere else.

The United States ranks third in daffodil bulb production. The majority of the industry is located in Washington, Oregon, and northern California, where the main concern is with cut-flower production rather than with bulb production in bulk.

Hubbard, Oregon, is the home of Grant Mitsch Novelty Daffodils, a daffodil farm established by our most renowned

More than two thousand cultivars at a glance in the collection of Cees Breed in Nordwijk, The Netherlands.

American hybridizer, Grant Mitsch. There his daughter, Elise Havens, and her husband Dick, continue to breed extraordinarily beautiful flowers. There are other growers in Oregon, too, who produce excellent-quality bulbs and hybrids (see "Sources for Bulbs"). The Pacific Northwest, with its cool, damp spring and dry summer, appears to be the ideal place to grow bulbs in the United States.

In the early part of the 20th century, Virginia was one of the largest producers of daffodils for cut flowers in the world. From the 1920s through the 1950s, a thousand or more acres were devoted to daffodil production. This area was even referred to as the "Daffodil Capital." But times, trends, and the industry changed. The popular cut flower once called the "poor man's rose" lost some of its popularity during the post-Depression years. Fields brimming with *Narcissus* were converted to corn, wheat, soybeans, and most recently, houses. Where millions of picked daffodils in tractor-trailer loads left the county daily in the spring, we now receive tractor-trailer loads of households of new residents.

There are only a couple of Virginia farms still raising daffodils for cut flowers and for limited production of bulbs. Our farm now is a 10-acre display garden and breeding farm where we evaluate thousands of cultivars and seedlings. We conduct trials of what we sell and provide tours and seminars for those wanting to learn more about these delightful flowers.

North Carolina still has several fairly large "pick flower" producers who market their bulbs primarily through mass market channels. A large grower there produces a number of our naturalizing type bulbs as well as some rare and unusual half-hardy bulbs that we carry.

There are a few other small, part-time businesses producing bulbs and fresh flowers for a limited market in various areas around the country. A number of specialty cut-flower producers are beginning to see the value of modern daffodils as a

Daffodils for cut-flower sales are picked just as the buds show color at Terra Ceia Farm in North Carolina.

profitable early spring crop. In the future, we expect to see more and better pick-flower daffodils and longer-lasting cultivars on the market. As freight prices increase, and as local produce and bulb products become more popular, bulb growing may once again become a strong enterprise around the United States.

Bulb growing is hard work but good exercise. The rewards for the small grower may be moderate financially, but they are large in the sensory pleasures and in the satisfaction from knowing that one is contributing something enjoyable to the world.

Daffodils will grow well in the shade if they get at least a half-day of sunlight and are fertilized annually.

II. Daffodil Anatomy

MONOCOTS

Because *Narcissus* seed germinates with just one embryonic seed leaf, it is classed as a monocotyledon, or monocot for short. Like other monocots, daffodils have elegant, straplike leaves with parallel veins, and the flower parts are always in threes or multiples of three. (Dicot flower parts, on the other hand, come in multiples of four or five.)

Daffodils are further divided into groups based on their unique shapes and multiples of parts. However, all species and cultivars of daffodils have this anatomy:

(Opposite) '*Delibes*' *and* '*Orange Emperor*' *are excellent perennial choices for the garden. Their complementary colors make them smashing companions.*

Root
Basal plate—the bottom portion of the bulb from which the roots emerge
Bulb
Stem or **scape**—the leafless flowering stalk
Leaves
Spathe—the semitransparent membrane enclosing the young flower bud and ovary
Flower
   Pedicel—neck
   Perianth—the six floral leaves
      Sepals—the three outer segments
      Petals—the three inner segments
   Corona—the cup, or trumpet-shaped disc-like outgrowth arising from the inner surface of the perianth at the base of the segments
   Pistil—female reproductive structure
      Stigma—the tip of the pistil that receives the pollen
      Style—the portion of the pistil connecting stigma and ovary
   Ovary—the swollen basal portion of the pistil, the part containing the ovules which after fertilization become the fruit containing the seeds. The ovary of the daffodil is divided into three sections, and it is inferior or below the perianth, which is characteristic of the Amaryllidaceae.
   Ovules—after fertilization become the seeds
   Stamen—male reproductive structure, one of the six pollen-bearing organs
      Anther—the terminal pollen-bearing part of the stamen
   Filament—the thin stalk of the stamen that supports the anther

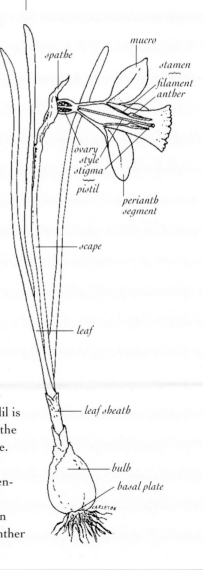

DRAWINGS PAGES 27 AND 28 BY PATRICIA CARLETON. COURTESY AMERICAN DAFFODIL SOCIETY

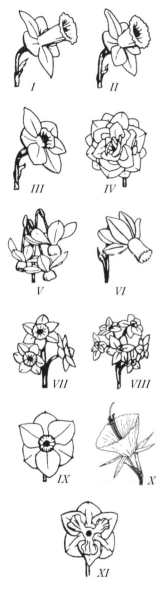

Illustrated above are some examples of characteristics that make each daffodil division unique.

THE THIRTEEN DIVISIONS OF DAFFODILS

The Royal Horticultural Society in England has established 13 official divisions of daffodils. Below is a summary of the characteristics of daffodils in each division.

Division I: *Trumpet Daffodils*
One flower to a stem. Corona (trumpet) as long as, or longer than, the perianth segments (petals).

Division II: *Large-Cupped Daffodils*
One flower to a stem. Corona (cup) more than one-third, but less than equal to, the length of the perianth segments (petals).

Division III: *Small-Cupped Daffodils*
One flower to a stem. Corona (cup) not more than one-third the length of the perianth segments (petals).

Division IV: *Double Daffodils*
One or more flowers to a stem, with doubling of the perianth segments or the corona or both.

Division V: *Triandrus Daffodils*
Usually two or more pendant flowers to a stem. Perianth segments (petals) are reflexed.

Division VI: *Cyclamineus Daffodils*
Usually one flower to a stem, perianth segments (petals) significantly reflexed. Flower at an acute angle to the stem, with a very short pedicel (neck).

Division VII: *Jonquilla Daffodils*
Usually one to five flowers to a stem. Perianth segments (petals) spreading or reflexed. Flowers fragrant.

Division VIII: *Tazetta Daffodils*
Usually 3–20 flowers to a stout stem. Perianth segments (petals) spreading, not reflexed. Flowers fragrant. Leaves broad.

Division IX: *Poeticus Daffodils*

Usually one flower to a stem. Perianth segments (petals) pure white. Corona usually disc-shaped, with a green or yellow center and a red rim. Flowers fragrant.

Division X: *Bulbocodium Daffodils*

Usually one flower to a stem. Perianth segments (petals) insignificant compared with corona. Filament and style are usually curved.

Division XI: *Split-Corona Daffodils*

Corona is split rather than lobed, usually split more than half its length.
a) Collar Daffodils – Split-corona daffodils with the corona segments opposite the perianth segments (petals). Corona segments usually in two whorls of three.
b) Papillon Daffodils – Split-corona daffodils with the corona segments alternate to the perianth segments (petals). Corona segments usually in a single whorl of six.

Division XII: *Other Daffodils*

All cultivars that do not fit the definition of any other division.

Division XIII: *Daffodils Distinguished Solely by Botanical name*

All species and wild or reputedly wild variants and hybrids.

BULB SIZES

The size of a daffodil bulb will often determine the number of blooms. A bulb's diameter is officially measured in centimeters. The diagram at right

(Top) A #1 grade double-nose bulb is compared in size to a #2 double-nose and a #3 round. (Bottom) A diagram of bulb sizes shows the circumference in centimeters and the diameter in inches.

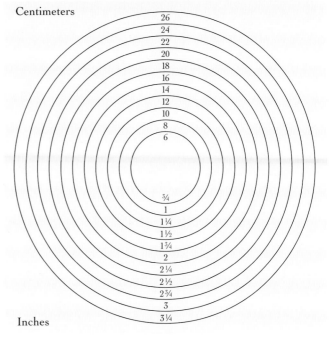

Centimeters

26
24
22
20
18
16
14
12
10
8
6

¾
1
1¼
1½
1¾
2
2¼
2½
2¾
3
3¼

Inches

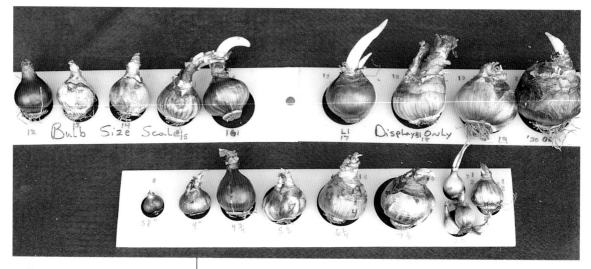

Bulb scales and bulbs illustrate the various sizes of bulbs from 6 cm to 18 cm.

includes the corresponding inch size.

Bulb sizes are given names in the trade. The official names are: #1 grade double-nose, often called "mother bulb" or " exhibition size" (which is a misnomer), featuring three noses or offsets and usually three or more blooms; #2 double-nose, often called "topsize" (also a misnomer) or "bedding size," featuring two or more blooms; #3 rounds, often called "#3 double-nose" (a misnomer), "landscape," or "naturalizing size," usually featuring one nose and one or more blooms. Rounds come in several sizes. Be sure to ask for the largest rounds unless you are looking for smaller planting stock. We find that they are the best size for uniform large blooms for forcing.

Generally speaking, the bulbs of trumpet, large cup, double, and split-corona daffodils should be the following measurements in diameter: #1 double-nose—20–24 cm (2 ½"–3"); #2 double-nose—16–20 cm (2"–2 ½"); and #3 round—12–18 cm (1 ½"–2 ¼").

For small cup, triandrus, cyclamineus, jonquilla, tazetta, and poeticus divisions, look for the following sizes: #1 double-nose—16–20 cm (2"–2 ½"); #2 double-nose—14–16 cm (1 ¾"–2"); and #3 round—10–16 cm (1 ⅓"–2").

Miniatures and species sizes vary greatly according to the type. *N. bulbocodium var. conspicuus* is usually 6-8 cm (¾"–1"). *N.* 'Tete-a-Tete' can be 10–16 cm (1 ¼"–2").

Each year the bulb is in the ground, it theoretically

doubles in number. The flower in the spring triggers a new growth bud at the basal plate that will form a daughter bulb or chip in the next growing season. As growing years ensue, the numbers grow from 1 to 2, to 4, 8, 16, 32, and 64. However, somewhere between 16 and 64 multiplication slows down and stops. As long as the growing cluster of bulbs receives enough sunlight, air, water, and nutrients, they will continue to bloom (see "Fertilizing").

The multiplication of bulbs is how there are enough in the world to sell. It takes a long time to bring a new cultivar to the market—the grower begins with just one bulb and must wait until it has multiplied into the thousands that it takes to offer it for sale. Many bulbs in the future will be multiplied by "parting," "chipping" or "twin scaling," which is a mechanized form of tissue culture that yields many times more than the normal increase. A large round bulb is cut into a number of pie-shaped pieces. Where the scales of these pieces meet the basal plate, bulblets form and grow into saleable large rounds after three years of special growing conditions. The parted rounds are of excellent quality and yield a large flower. Some cultivars are offered in parted rounds only. The parted round that you plant this year should be a double-nose next year, if you provide good growing conditions.

Daffodils are considered seedlings until the flower is selected to be "better" or "different" and given a name.

An interesting phenomenon with newly purchased bulbs is that they will often bloom one to two weeks later than bulbs of the same variety already in the ground. This happens because summers are cooler in Holland and England where most commercial bulbs are grown, and the bulbs mature later and therefore bloom later.

III. Daffodil Culture

The daffodil might be considered the ideal perennial. It survives in all but the hottest areas (climatic zone 10) and the coldest (zones 2 and 3). In the majority of areas in the United States and southern and coastal Canada, it thrives and perennializes. The daffodil is tolerant of most soils having adequate drainage, and it flourishes in sandy loam. It's drought-tolerant in all seasons except spring. It's almost pest-free and has simple nutritional requirements. It's an excellent companion plant for perennials, annuals, ground covers, shrubs, and trees.

WHEN TO PLANT

The best time to plant is in the fall when the ground temperature (at a depth of 6"–8") is at or below 60°F, usually around the date of the first frost or when trees begin to lose their leaves. To measure the soil temperature, dig a hole 8" deep in your garden area, insert a soil thermometer or a standard room thermometer upright in the earth, and wait five minutes. To foster the best root growth, it's important that the soil temperature not be higher than 60°F.

If it's February or March and you still haven't planted your bulbs, plant them as soon as possible provided that the bulbs are still firm. Flowers from late-planted bulbs, if they don't abort, will bloom later than normal and will have shorter stems, although the bulbs will catch up in a year or two. Don't expect to store your old bulbs to keep until the following fall. No bulb is engineered to stay out of the ground that long. They'll dry out!

WHERE TO PLANT

In the wild, many species *Narcissus* prefer the sloping habitats of hillsides or mountains, where natural drainage is excellent. These areas generally receive a fair amount of rainfall while the bulbs are growing but become fairly dry during the bulb's dormant season. Because daffodil hybrids include an inheritance of characteristics from species *Narcissus*, bulbs perform better when planted in elevated areas.

Few of us have steep hillsides to offer our bulbs, so we

(Opposite) *The stark white of the 'Ice Wings' daffodil shows off well against the dark blue color of* Muscari armeniacum *'Blue Spike' and pansies.* (Above) *St. Mary's Church created a raised bed to make a suitable planting site for their bulbs, which joyfully greet the congregation each Sunday morning in spring.*

A brick wall will give wind and winter protection to Narcissus jonquilla, *which benefits from summer baking and a southern exposure.*

need to create little hills in the form of berms, or raised beds. Those of us dealing with fairly heavy, poorly drained, clay soil types will find it especially important to raise the level of the soil bed for optimum growth conditions.

When choosing your garden site, keep in mind that most daffodils prefer full sun, but most will tolerate half shade, whether as filtered light all day long or as hours of shade before or after hours of sunshine. If your garden will be near a shade tree, notice how much sunlight filters through the leaves. There should be at least half a day of sunshine available for your flowers.

Try to locate your flower bed where your normal routine will bring you walking by it each day or where you and your family will see it when you look out a window. Try to put your garden where friends and neighbors will see and enjoy it, too. There's nothing more rewarding than being congratulated on a beautiful garden by appreciative visitors!

After you've chosen your garden site, the next step is to create a bulb bed with good soil texture. You do not need to dig up the soil to a 12" or 14" depth. Instead, build up the bulb bed from grade level with humus-rich soil (see "Soils and Soil Amendments" and "Cultural Recommendations by Region"). The humus-rich soil aids in water retention during drought periods, and the raised bed helps wet soil to drain properly — two ingredients for successful flower beds.

Now to select your bulbs. Plant selection is one of the most exciting parts of creating a bed or border. Consult the sections "In the Company of Daffs" and "Recommended Daffodils in Commercial Culture" for ideas on companion plants and daffodil cultivars. In flower beds bulbs should be planted in groups of at least 10 or more for the group to achieve a good focal effect. Try not to place many limits on yourself. Nature limits our bulb choices to some extent, in terms of cold hardiness and tolerance to heat, but if you've ever been to Hurricane Ridge in Washington state or to other alpine meadows in the summer, you know that nature places no limits on juxtaposing colors! Remember, too, that you're not planting in concrete: you can change your mind and move things around later if you want.

Once prepared, your beds should rise about 6"–8" above the surrounding site. Extra elevation in the center of the berm serves to show off your bulbs to better advantage. If your bed is larger than five square feet, the soil should be gradually sloped upward until the center is 5"–10" higher than the edges of the berm. Flowers in the center of the berm will be more visually prominent than if they'd been planted in a flat bed.

Some of the berm elevation can be easily set up by applying thick mulches to the height you want (see "Mulch"). Keep in mind that bulb roots need 6"–8" of good soil underneath them as that is where the roots will find their sustenance. The quality of the soil on top of your bulbs is not as important as long as it's not compacted and bulbs can push up through it easily.

If you have limited time or funds, you can begin a bulb garden as just a small border or edge planting. Expand your border a little more every year. You'll probably find that your experience with the first bulbs has given you ideas for the next year's display.

SOILS AND SOIL AMENDMENTS

The ideal soil for daffodil bulbs is a deep, rich sandy loam with plenty of well-decomposed organic matter. About 10% to 20% of us in the United States are blessed with a soil situation close to the ideal. The rest of us find that with a small investment in materials and time, we can amend our heavier clay or lighter sandy soils to create a nearly ideal bed for our bulbs.

Heavy clay soils, composed of fine soil particles that can become compacted, can be a serious problem when you're first establishing the bed. If drainage is extremely poor, you might consider installing gravel in deep post holes or perforated drainpipe below the root level. Contact your USDA county extension agent for more information on drainage methods.

Most heavy soils can be amended effectively simply by mixing in equal amounts of organic matter and coarse builder's sand. The best organic matter is well-decomposed compost.

However, if you're using compost, prepare the bed at least a couple of months before you plant. The soil particles need time to mingle with the compost and microbes need time to break down the organic matter so that nutrients will be available to the bulbs. Delay of a month or two between preparing the bed and planting the bulbs assures that the compost will be totally decomposed, with little risk of leftover bacterial heat that can initiate rot in the bulbs.

ORGANIC SOIL AMENDMENTS

Well-decomposed compost. Comprised of household and yard waste that has had complete aerobic decomposition (i.e., complete breakdown of plant tissues in the presence of plenty of air to produce good humus and nutrients).

Leaf compost. Finely ground and decomposed leaf matter works best if lime (calcium carbonate) and balanced fertilizer are mixed in, along with other organic compost.

Finely ground pine bark. An excellent amendment that is readily available in bagged form, often labeled as "Soil Conditioner." This type of amendment decomposes slowly and lasts much longer in the soil than does peat moss, which breaks down quickly and leaves little residue.

Composted sewage sludge. "Milorganite" or "Nutra Green" (or other local labels) is municipal sewage sludge that has been composted with wood chips to make a humus-rich soil amendment. Milorganite and Nutra Green both have certification of testing for freedom from pathogens and heavy metals. In our opinion, this is the best single organic amendment available to create the nearly ideal bulb bed. To create the perfect bed, we would combine the first four items on this list.

Well-composted horse, chicken, or cow manure, or mushroom compost. A good source of organic matter. Please make sure that any of these has been composted long enough that the heat has gone out of it. Small doses in addition to other amendments is best.

Sharp builders sand. A coarse grade of sharp sand is usually available from building suppliers. Sand opens up the soil texture, which in turn improves drainage. Remember that builders sand is not the same as finer grained sand from the seashore.

HOW TO PLANT YOUR DAFFODILS

Depth and Proximity

Bulb planting is an enjoyable exercise provided it's done properly with adequate tools and good teamwork. Without those, it can be a source of "bulb planters elbow" or blisters on the palm of your hand.

Most larger bulbs (2"–3" in diameter) should be planted at a depth (at the bottom of the hole) of three to four times the height of the bulb. In general, then, plant the large bulbs 6"–8" deep, depending on your soil type. Heavy, clay soils require shallower planting, light soils a bit deeper.

Medium-sized bulbs (1"–2" in diameter) should be planted at a depth of 3"–6." Small or miniature bulbs (½"–1" in diameter) should be planted 2"–3" deep.

As for how far apart to plant bulbs: three times the width of the bulb is the general rule about distance.

Plant the bulb base down, with its "nose" upward. If you accidently plant a bulb sideways or upside down, the daffodil's strong contractile roots will eventually pull the bulb into upright position and the shoot will grow upward. However, this will cost your plant both time and energy, so it's better to take a moment to insert the bulb upright when you plant.

Proper Tools

The proper tool can make or break your day of planting. Unfortunately the two tools most often sold for bulb planting are cheaply made and adequate only in the best soils and only if you have a few bulbs to plant. Good tools are more of an investment but can help to make your bulb planting a pleasurable activity.

A tool called the "Heavy Duty Bulb Planter" comes with a 3"-diameter, 10"-deep stainless-steel cone, large enough to

A team working with the Naturalizing Tool to plant bulbs in an unprepared site can easily plant thousands of bulbs in a day.

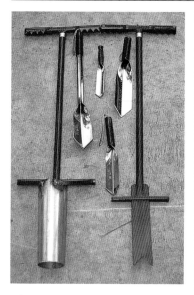

The Heavy Duty Bulb Planter with its stainless steel tube is designed for use in prepared soil, while the Naturalizing Tool is made for plugging bulbs in unprepared soil and ground covers. Hand trowels work most effficiently if the handles fit your hand and the blade fits the size of the specific bulb to be planted.

accommodate the largest daffodil bulb and excellent for plugging holes when you're planting annuals or perennials. Its 1" steel frame and T-handle make it a lifetime tool. Two people, one plugging holes in well-prepared soil, the other placing bulbs in the new holes, can plant 3,000 to 4,000 bulbs a day.

Place the Heavy Duty Bulb Planter on the spot to be excavated, step on the crossbar to push it into soil, twist the T-handle to free the plug, then pull up with the plug of soil inside the planter. Do not dump out the plug. When you repeat the process, the second plug will push the first plug out through the top of the planter. Your partner places bulbs in the holes and covers the bulbs with plugs from the previous holes.

There are several intermediate-sized versions of this tool to excavate somewhat smaller plugs. These tools work well for smaller bulbs and smaller quantities of bulbs.

Then there is the lightweight version that is chrome-plated with a 2" tube. This is fine for use with just a few small bulbs in ideal soil. However, this tool will break at the neck if used in heavy soil or for a large number of bulbs. In our estimation this tool is a waste of money. Pay twice as much for a heavier, reliable implement. You can always rent it to or share it with your neighbors.

There are several grades and models available of the handheld tubular planter. This tool is an excellent candidate for "blistermaker" if you use it in heavy soil or for more than about 100 bulbs. A good sturdy trowel is a much better investment.

The "Naturalizing Tool" is one of the best all-purpose planting tools that you can own. It resembles a narrow spade: it has a 3"-wide, 8"-long sharp blade, a truck spring attached to a 1" steel pipe shaft, a foot bar, and a T-handle. This tool enables you to plant bulbs in prepared or unprepared soil, in ground covers, and amongst the roots of trees and shrubs.

To use the Naturalizing Tool, you can either thrust the tool into the soil by hand or step on the footbar to insert the tool. Then pull back on the handle about 30° to lift a small hump of soil in front of the tool. Step on the footbar to anchor the tool and push the bar away from you to move the hump of soil aside, forming a 3" x 8" slot for a planting hole. Your partner drops the bulb in the hole and steps on the hump of soil to push it around the bulb. Working together, two people can insert 3,000 to 4,000 bulbs in a good day, provided they have good soil without many rocks or roots.

Bulb trowels are a series of stainless steel tools manufactured for multiple uses. They are ideal for planting large quantities of small bulbs or small quantities of large bulbs. The technique for using the 9" x 1" small bulb trowel is to consider it a dagger. Stab the trowel into the soil to a depth of 3". Pull the trowel toward you about 1"–2" to open a hole. Drop in the bulb, then stab the ground at a spot about 2"–3" away and pull the trowel toward you again, covering the first hole and creating the second. Using this "stab-pull-drop" method in well-prepared soil, an experienced gardener can plant 500–1,000 little bulbs per hour.

The larger bulb trowel is ideal for the home gardener who has a few hundred bulbs to plant. The method of use is similar to that for the smaller trowel: stab the soil, pull back on the handle, push a little deeper to widen the hole, drop in the bulb, stab again, and the second hole covers the first.

We do not recommend the dibble method of planting as the dibble compresses the soil and makes it more difficult for the bulbs to root. We feel that hand excavation of beds for bulb planting, without using tools designed for the job, is a waste of time and energy. Mechanical excavation with large equipment may save time, but has the tendency to compact soils.

(Upper) *The tubular planter works best when you let one plug push another out of the top of the planter. Concrete reinforcing wire makes an excellent 6" template for spacing bulbs.*
(Lower) *A large stainless steel trowel treated like a dagger is the best way to plant fewer than 100 large bulbs in prepared soil.*

WATER

The moisture needs of daffodil bulbs are heavy and critical during the spring growing season, virtually nonexistent during summer dormancy, light and steady during fall root initiation, and light throughout the winter. During the growing season, March through May, the bulbs will perform best if they receive ½"–1" of moisture every week. More than ½"–1" of water during the weeks of April and May would be a waste. Please do not overwater!

Where supplemental irrigation is required, it is best supplied by a form of drip irrigation rather than by overhead spray. Drip irrigation provides a steady amount of moisture over an extended period of time at a rate easily usable by the bulbs. Drip irrigation also keeps the foliage from being weighed down by too much water and saves flowers from being splattered and water-marked.

Depending on the dryness of your climate and your type of watering equipment, you might want to consider special amendments to increase the soil's water-holding capacity. One is a polymer, "Supersorb," whose granules, when mixed deep in the soil in the root zone of the bed, form a gel that retains water. This gelled water gradually passes back to the plants during dry spells. Another possible amendment is a ceramic granule made from diatomaceous earth. This material absorbs and stores water, then releases the water gradually.

MULCH

Mulch is the hero that saves the daffodil bulb garden. When properly applied, it controls undesirable weeds, conserves moisture, and keeps the beds cool under shade in the heat of summer. Mulch can even take the place of topsoil if bulbs have to be planted where the soil texture is poor or soil drainage inadequate. You can improve any topsoil by adding organic matter to a depth of 8". In a poor soil, when bulbs are planted 2"–3" deep and given 6" of mulch as a top cover, a good root zone is provided for the bulbs and drainage is also improved because you've created a kind of raised bed.

Pine straw (or "needles," "pine tags," "pine shats," or whatever it's called in your area) is one of the best mulches. It's light, airy, attractive, and it does not tend to float off in rainfall or blow away in a breeze. If applied thickly enough (at least 2"), it suppresses weed growth.

Pine bark is another excellent mulch possibility. It has all the virtues of pine straw with only one minor drawback: when

'Jetfire' daffodils and pansies grow happily through pine straw mulch.

pine bark is kept moist, weed seeds blowing in can germinate and grow. Medium-sized nuggets (½"–1" in diameter) tend to bind together loosely and are best to use. Larger chunks of bark, from 1"–3" in diameter, tend to become dislodged and float away during heavy rains. Look for mulch with a low percentage of cellulose (wood chips) as this tends

'St. Keverne' makes a great display when planted in mass. Here it is shown surrounded by pine bark, an excellent mulch for daffodils.

to rob the soil of nitrogen when it's breaking down. Using a high-cellulose mulch may mean you'll have to increase your nitrogen fertilization later on.

Well-ground hardwood mulch whose fibers have been broken into pieces about ½"–1" in diameter also makes a fine mulch. Be aware that ungraded mulch may have large fibrous chunks in it, around which your bulbs may find it difficult to emerge. Hardwood mulch also tends to grow fungus which then can form solid mats.

Pea gravel, volcanic stone, and similar products are excellent mulch, particularly in gardens where species and miniature type bulbs are used. Buckwheat hulls, cocoa hulls, and other seed hulls have good reputations as garden mulch.

We do not recommend using black plastic or landscape fabric as a mulch. Bulbs are not able to emerge through these materials. It has been our experience that even when Xs are cut into the fabric, bulb growth and emergence are not satisfactory.

FERTILIZING

A bulb is a plant storage organ to provide nutrition to the growing foliage and flower as well as to collect and store starches for the plant's future nutrition needs. Applying fertilizers is our attempt to replenish the soil with the nutrients and minerals necessary for the bulb's production of starches and sugars.

The simplest and best bulb fertilizer is good soil rich in humus and other organic matter. Supplemental minerals and nutritional elements, applied periodically, can help keep clumps of bulbs blooming indefinitely.

Once your bulbs have been planted and watered in cool soil (below 60°F), the roots initiate growth. As they fan out and anchor the bulbs, the roots interact with soil particles around them and begin to absorb nutrients and minerals. This process takes place slowly in the fall and almost ceases after the soil is frozen. The process restarts in early spring, continues through late spring, then ceases until the following fall. As bulbs multiply in a given spot, they begin to use up the supply of soil nutrients around them. Blooming will cease when a root system is no longer able to assimilate sufficient nutrients for the leaves to use in photosynthetic production of sugars and starches.

With the foretold story in mind, it is easier to understand the necessity of supplemental top dressing of nutrients in the fall to keep your established bulbs in top condition. The top-dressed fertilizer will have a chance to leach gradually in and attach to soil particles. We do not recommend putting fertilizer in the planting hole with a bulb because of the risk that tender new roots will be burned and dried by the fertilizer as it dissolves.

The following spring, you can topdress with fertilizer if you forgot to do it in the fall. We recommend a water-soluble formula such as (5-11-26) as a spring fertilizer to be applied between emergence and blooming time. Top dressing with a nonwater-soluble fertilizer after the spring is usually considered a waste of material because the nutrients are not likely to work their way down to the root zone in time to do any good for this season.

If your soil is deficient in phosphorous, you may want to incorporate extra phosphorus into the soil at planting time because phosphorous travels downward slowly in most soils, only about 1" per year, whereas nitrogen, potassium, and most

Pink- or salmon-cupped daffodil 'Romance' shares a bed with late, double, pink tulip 'Angelique'.

other minerals leach into the soil readily with normal rainfall or irrigation. The better the organic content of the soil, the more readily available any nutrient will be to your plants.

Bonemeal used to be considered the ideal bulb fertilizer until research at North Carolina State University indicated that bonemeal has little nitrogen, almost no potassium, and only a fair amount of phosphorus and calcium. Think of bonemeal for bulbs as comparable to your own consumption of broccoli: it's nutritious but not a complete source of nutrients.

We think the ideal organic formula, made of all naturally occurring ingredients, is "Bulb Mate," a formula by Bricker Company that contains cricket manure, rock phosphate, bone meal, dolomitic limestone, granite meal, and organic compost. It has a 5-10-12 formula (5% nitrogen, 10% potash, 12% potassium).

In our opinion the ideal manufactured fertilizer for daffodils is the slow-release "Daffodil Fertilizer." It has a 5-10-20 formula and also contains trace amounts of manganese, iron, copper, sulphur, boron, and zinc and is available from Brent and Becky's Bulbs. Slow-release products gradually release nutrients at approximately the rate of use by the bulbs and generally for the length of time that bulbs need more nutrients.

Other possible fertilizers are those generally called *bulb fertilizers*. These are adequate if used in sequential doses and with the addition of extra potash, as most of these fertilizers do not have as much potassium as daffodil bulbs typically use. "Holland Bulb Booster" is an excellent slow-release fertilizer formulated for tulips and members of the lily family. It's fine for daffodils, too, if one is willing to supplement it with extra potash.

Among the excellent organic sources of potash is wood ash, which also contains trace elements needed by bulbs. Wood ash has an alkaline pH and can help to neutralize acidic soils. Apply wood ash only once per season and avoid using it near woody evergreens since those prefer a higher soil acidity and might turn yellow with chlorosis as a result of potash supplements.

Another organic source of potash is "New Jersey Green-

Identifying the perennial daffodils that best tolerate a partially shaded, woodland setting in Westchester County, NY.

We used to think violets were weeds until N. 'Foundling' bloomed with them – and looked better than ever!

sand," a marine deposit of potash and trace elements from the Delaware Valley. This product is mined and then distributed by several organic fertilizer suppliers.

Several chemically derived sources such as muriate of potash and sulfate of potash are available in varying concentrations. Please be cautious when using these. These are products that can leach through soils to the water table. If too strong in concentration these chemicals can burn plant roots and pollute the environment.

A soil pH of slightly acid to neutral is ideal for most *Narcissus* (check "Recommended Daffodils in Commercial Culture" for cultivars preferring a more acid soil). Daffodils tend to be tolerant of everything except extremes. If you're not sure about the pH of your soil, most city or county extension offices of the USDA offer soil testing kits that can be ordered and used easily.

Here's a color tip about fertilizing: applying ½ cup of magnesium sulfate (Epsom salts) per 10 square feet in the fall or early spring, sprinkled as a top dressing over your bulbs, is thought to increase the intensity of color in daffodil flowers, particularly in the red and pink range.

Another tip: in the spring, mark with golf tees the area of bulbs that will need fertilizing in the fall. Set the tees in a circle around the clump. That way you can come back in the fall and know where to spread the fertilizer. Another way to mark your plantings is to use Muscari, whose foliage emerges in the fall. Planting Muscari around other daffodil plantings will give you a quick way to find buried bulbs for future fertilization.

WEEDING

The most effective weed prevention is a good layer of mulch (see the "Mulch" section, above). Another way to help control weeds is to fill your flower beds with so many plants that there isn't much room for weeds to take hold. This means more color and less maintenance! Another effective weed-control method, one that's not nearly so pretty, is the use of herbicides.

Pre-emergent herbicides inhibit the germination of certain

weeds and grasses but do not effect the emergence of bulbs. Please be cautious and frugal with these products if you choose to use them. We feel that many of the environmental pollution problems in the United States and Canada come directly from you and me, from our cumulative use of household and garden chemicals.

There are several pre-emergent herbicides registered for use with daffodils. Contact your USDA county extension agent for advice on what is registered for use and available in your area.

There are also a number of post-emergent herbicides that can be used over planted daffodils once their foliage has withered away in late spring. We prefer to use herbicides that decompose into natural compounds when they mix with soil. "Roundup" is such a product, and it is effective and biodegradable. However, be careful during its application: Roundup will systemically kill any green plant tissue with which it comes into contact.

Of course, the best weed control of all is your own hands. We enjoy weeding for a little while every day. That keeps the weeds at bay, and we get the bonus of seeing our plants in closeup. It's only when you don't weed regularly that weeding becomes a chore.

INSECTS AND DISEASES

The dearth of insect problems and disease makes members of the Amaryllis family, of which *Narcissus* is a major part, one of the most popular pest-free perennials for the garden. Only a few insects and nematodes are able to withstand the poisonous alkaloid in the daffodil bulbs and foliage.

Lesser bulb flies and bulb scale mites are generally found only after the bulb has been injured and is beginning to decompose. But a creature called the Narcissus bulb fly is sometimes encountered in old plantings where the fly has been able to propagate. Sometimes when you're digging up old clumps of bulbs you'll find one with a small, shiny white offset near the base, or with a hole the size of a BB in the base of the bulb, or a bulb with a soft neck. These are signs of a large bulb fly

N. *'Quail' is very much at home in a bed of* Euphorbia polychroma.

larva (maggot) inside. If you think the bulb is worth salvaging, make a small incision and fish out the maggot with a sharp pick.

Carefully check all your dug bulbs and, as a rule, discard all infested ones. As a preventive measure late in the blooming season, pull off yellowing foliage and cover the resulting holes with soil or mulch. If and when the rarity of a bad infestation occurs, check with your USDA county extension agent for recommendations about systemic insecticides. No insecticide is specifically registered for *Narcissus*, but any insecticide registered for onion root maggot will do the job.

Other preventive measures for the Narcissus bulb fly involve you and a butterfly net. Near the end of the blooming season, on a day of about 70°F, station yourself near some daffodils and catch the large yellow and brown flies that resemble honeybees with only one set of wings and make a loud buzzing noise. This is also great exercise!

A more important problem for daffodils is fungal disease called basal rot caused by *Fusarium oxysporum f. narcissi*. If your bulbs do not come up, they may have succumbed to the disease. Signs of basal rot among stored bulbs include a white band around the basal plate, brown streaks on the bulb's side, soft texture, and rotten smell. Fungus can be avoided by proper cultural practices and proper varietal selection. The two most important factors to remember are good drainage and, in warmer climates such as zones 6 through 9, providing summer shade over the bulbs (see "Companion Plantings").

If you've lost bulbs to fungus, do not plant other bulbs in the same location for several seasons or until you've treated the infected soil with "Terra Chlor," a soil fungicide, to kill off remaining spores. You might choose to have your soil fumigated in the summer using a clear plastic tarp that heats the tilled soil beneath it and kills the fungal spores. There is also a preplanting dip, a systemic fungicide that can help ward off fungus attacks if they've become a problem in your area.

Another pest, nematodes, or microscopic eel worms, leave brown necrotic rings in the tissues of a bulb and small white bumps or speckles on the leaves. The leaves and flowers often become distorted and stunted. The best methods of control are

(Opposite) *'Beryl' is a graceful, intermediate-sized daffodil that perennializes well.*

the use of systemic nematocides as well as fumigation of the area surrounding the infected bulbs. Marigolds grown over the beds help to eradicate nematodes. Fortunately, the eel worm problem is seldom encountered in home gardens.

Early in the 20th century the nematode *Ditylenchus dipsaci* created havoc for a while in the bulb industry. But with the development by commercial growers of a hot-water treatment, nematodes have been virtually eliminated as a bulb pest.

One other daffodil disease that sometimes occurs is a series of viruses manifested as variegation in the color of the foliage. These viruses will weaken the bulb but seldom kill it. They are spread by aphids feeding on the foliage or by soil-borne nematodes (different from the harmful nematodes that feed on the bulbs). The control method is to rogue, or dig out, all affected plants and dispose of them.

Fortunately for the home gardener, these pests seldom become a problem. Most bulb growers are responsible and conscientious about keeping their stock clean and in the best of health. If you buy from a reputable grower, avoid bargain bulbs whose price is too good to be true, plant your bulbs in good, well-drained soil, and fertilize properly, your daffodils should not encounter any pests or diseases.

DEADHEADING THE BLOOMS AND MATURING FOLIAGE

The benefits of picking off the dead flower heads are negligible. Unlike tulips that use up to 30% of their energy making seeds, very few hybrid daffodils are pollinated in the garden. Hybrids are not self-pollinating like some of the species *Narcissus*; the pollen is too heavy to be windborne; and few insects visit the flowers because they contain little nectar. More likely than not, if the flower is left on and a fat seedpod appears, it will be empty, the sign of a false pregnancy. There is one exception: sometimes a bumblebee will seek overnight refuge in the cup or trumpet of a large daffodil and fertilize it.

However, you may want to deadhead for aesthetic reasons when the beautiful flowers begin to fade. Snap off the spent flower head at the neck, leaving the stem to act as another leaf for photosynthesis.

A more serious concern is how to handle the maturing foliage of the daffodils. Many old gardening publications suggest that it is acceptable to braid the leaves or bend them over and secure them with a rubber band to tidy up the garden. These practices are detrimental to the daffodil's growth and storage of sufficient starches for the next year's bloom. The foliage needs sunlight and oxygen in order to photosynthesize properly. Bunching the foliage cuts off sunlight, suffocates the leaves, and causes fungal problems.

It is aesthetically pleasing to deadhead dying blossoms but only culturally beneficial if they have been pollinated. Most hybrids are not pollinated by insects.

It is far better to plan your plantings to have companions emerge and mask the maturing foliage of the bulbs (see "Companion Planting"). In planning the visual effect of a garden, we consider the wide foliage of daffodils a linear effect. If this type of foliage is not appealing to you, the divisions 5–10 (triandus through species) tend to have smaller, thinner foliage, and you may want to choose from these groups.

When the foliage begins to turn yellow and fall over, it is losing its chlorophyll and will soon no longer serve the bulb. This is the time to cut the foliage. If the bulbs have been well watered and fertilized, we suggest that you wait at least eight to ten weeks after bloom before cutting the foliage.

DIGGING BULBS

The best time to dig your daffodil bulbs, regardless of the cultivar, is when the foliage has begun to turn yellow and collapse. By that time the plant's photosynthesis process to manufacture carbohydrates for next year's flowers has ceased. If you dig at this time, the foliage will still be visible and the bulbs easy to locate, which means less chance of your accidentally piercing or slicing a bulb.

We are sometimes asked whether bulbs can be dug while they're in bloom. It's possible, of course, but the fact is that during the blooming period the bulb is in the middle of its normal growth cycle. We like to compare it to the birth of a baby. Many babies survive and some are healthy when the normal gestation period is interrupted by early birth, but those who survive usually have to struggle to catch up in growth. The same is true with bulbs. We always recommend that you wait through the growth period. If you're moving and the only time you can dig is in the middle of the blooming period, then perhaps the risk is worthwhile. Remember that it might take a couple of years for your bulbs to recover from the shock of being jerked out of place during their development period.

As we explained under "Fertilizing," it's a good idea in the spring to insert golf tees in a circle around the area where your bulbs are growing. Then you won't have the experience of being unable to find your bulbs when the foliage has gone and there's no clear sign where to dig.

Cured or dried bulbs store best in a dry, well-ventilated area in containers such as wire trays or mesh bags.

When you dig your bulbs, dig around and underneath the bulbs with a fork or spade. Try not to cut the bulbs or to break many roots. Shake off the dirt and untangle the roots gently. If two bulbs are firmly attached to one another, don't break them apart as this may injure them both and cause them to rot. When replanted, the attached bulb will split off from the mother bulb when the time is right.

If you know where you intend to replant the bulbs you've dug, you might plant them again the same day you dig; in fact, we recommend this. But if you must store your dug bulbs, then dry them thoroughly. Provide good circulation (a fan is useful) to dry the bulbs on all sides. The mesh bags used in grocery stores for onions or fruit are good storage containers as they allow air circulation around and between the bulbs.

It's also a good idea to mark your calendar for the future planting day. We get a lot of "Help!" calls in March from customers who just found the bulbs in the garage, the bulbs they dug last summer and forgot to replant!

CULTURAL RECOMMENDATIONS BY REGION

Northeastern United States and Canada

The Northeast, encompassing New England, northeastern Canada, and parts of New York, New Jersey, and Pennsylvania, provides one of the most successful habitats for daffodils. In this part of the United States is one of the largest populations of daffodil fanciers. The cold winters and moderate spring weather are excellent for almost all daffodils except some of the more tender tazetta hybrids. Planting in early fall so the bulbs can make good root growth before the ground freezes is most important. Plant at least six weeks before the ground freezes hard, any time after the ground temperature at a depth of 6" has dropped to 60°F. Mulch the new plantings well to insulate against cold in the first year. If it's a dry fall, water the new plantings well.

Trumpet and poeticus daffodils are at their best in these cooler climates. There seem to be fewer fungal problems than in warmer areas. Making use of microclimates for site selection can be important to coax earlier bloom. You might choose areas near fences and hedges to offer protection from harsh weather and wind. The one drawback to the climate of the northeast is that you have to wait so long for spring. If we lived up there, we'd force a good selection of bulbs all winter long to remind us that spring is on the way!

Mid-Atlantic

This central seaboard region has been touted as one of the best daffodil areas in the country. With our temperate climate here, we have the best of both worlds, cool and warm. We have the largest number of daffodil enthusiasts and some of the country's largest and finest daffodil shows. Because our winters are normally mild, our growing season can be long, often lasting 8–12 weeks. If we stretch the season from plantings of *N.* 'Rijnveld's Early Sensation,' which blooms here in January, to the *N. poeticus* var. *recurvus*, which blooms in May, we can get four months of continuous bloom. Our only shortcoming might be that our area sometimes gets too warm too early in April and May so that we're a bit short on moisture

The USDA Plant Hardiness Zone Map on page 140 will help you determine in which plant zone you live. This information is beneficial when selecting plant material.

when the plants are really thirsty in late spring. But with a little planning and a small expenditure, we can insure enough water by installing drip irrigation (see "Water").

Here we need to plan on planting our bulbs from about mid-October up through November for best results. However, in most years we can safely plant bulbs until Christmas. Earlier planting results in better root growth and better overall performance. Later-blooming cultivars, such as the cupped, pink and red varieties, should be positioned to receive partial shade to protect their fragile colors from the midday sun.

Companion planting, too, is important in our region to provide shade for the bulbs during the hot and humid summers. We often use sunflowers as our main cover crop. The use of vegetables (particularly melons, squash, and cucumbers) also gives excellent summer shade. Plants growing above the bulbs use up the available moisture and keep the bulbs relatively dry. Berm or elevated-bed planting is important in our climate because basal rot fungus can become a problem during humid summers in spots that lack good drainage.

We sometimes find that bulbs in this region begin to emerge in the fall. We get a few frantic phone calls every fall from people asking us what to do. We jokingly say to push them back down. We go on to explain that some light mulch around the new shoots will help protect them and that daffodils are actually pretty tough. They can sustain temperatures down to the single digits without ill effect.

'Avalanche' or "Seventeen Sisters" is an ideal bulb for mid-Atlantic gardens like Monticello, Thomas Jefferson's home in Charlottesville, Virginia.

Southeast

The Southeast is a good area for growing some types of daffodils, ideal for others, and poor for a few types. It's an ideal place for the tender tazetta types and their relatives, as well as for any other types from warmer regions such as jonquilla relatives and some of the species bulbs. The early bloomers tend to do pretty well because their growth activity peaks when the temperature is cooler, in the very early spring. The foliage has time to rejuvenate the sugars stored in the bulb while the weather stays relatively cool.

Generally speaking, the trumpets, poeticus, doubles, and white daffodils (except jonquilla and tazetta types) do not fare well in the Southeast except under special protected circumstances. Most other daffodils do well if several precautions are taken. Good drainage and summer shading are the two most important requirements. Basal rot is probably the single worst affliction, but you can prevent this or reduce its incidence by making sure your bulbs don't stay wet for long during the summer. Plant them in elevated beds. Do not irrigate the bulbs in the summer months. Plant crops over the bulbs to shade them and to use up summer moisture so the bulbs stay dry. Our customers in the Deep South (zones 8 and 9) tell us that 'Carlton,' 'Gigantic Star,' and 'St. Keverne' are the best big yellow cultivars for that warm climate, whereas most large yellow daffodils wither away in the heat.

A massive sweep of daffodils makes quite a show in many Southeastern landscapes like Barnsley Gardens in Adairsville, Georgia.

North-Central United States and Canada

The north-central area of the United States and Canada has some of the coldest temperatures and sometimes the shortest spring season. The first three divisions and the poeticus thrive under these conditions. Many of the other divisions also grow well, with the exception of the tazettas. Tazettas may need a microclimate or some extra protection. We have had customers tell us they plant hardy tazettas on the south side of the house and up against the foundation. That gives them enough protection to withstand the often severe winter temperatures.

However, we have had other customers from the same climate zone say that planting tazettas out in their regular garden area helps the bulbs to acclimate and toughen up. They believe that planting tazettas in a protected area encourages them to bloom too early, when they'll get nipped by hard freezes in late winter. To us it sounds as if experimentation is in order for the questionable cultivars. Of course, successful planting will depend on the lowest temperature of the particular winter and on whether there was snow cover. We've been assured that it's well worth the risk of loss to have the fragrance of tazettas in the garden.

Early planting from mid-September to mid-October is essential to success in this region. Watering after planting is important as bulbs will not initiate roots in dry soil. Bulbs that have not rooted by the time the ground freezes may be lost. In this climate, mulching is beneficial to keep the soil a more uniform temperature and give added protection to the bulbs. Seek out protected microclimates and enjoy your flowers over a longer period of time. Include plenty of late-blooming cultivars to extend your season.

Midcentral and Great Plains

The midcentral states of Ohio, Indiana, southern Illinois, Kentucky, Tennessee, and eastern Missouri normally have adequate rainfall; long, cool springs; and winters and summers that aren't terribly extreme. That explains why this section of the United States hosts some of the loveliest daffodil gardens and displays. You may need to find microclimates to success-fully grow some of the more tender *tazettas*, but the rest of the divisions will grow and bloom beautifully.

The Great Plains region has some of the most fertile soils in the country and also some of the worst extremes in weather. Usually there is a brief spring at the end of a cold winter and then the arrival of a long, hot summer. Rainfall is usually adequate and sometimes over-abundant.

Plant your bulbs in both warm and cool microclimates in order to extend the season. Plant usually after October 1, when the soil has cooled down to 60°F at a depth of 6". White daffodils and other cultivars susceptible to basal rot do not fare well during the hot, humid summers of the Great Plains unless the bulbs are shaded in elevated plantings.

South-Central

The south-central or Gulf Coast region and the area just north of it present more of a challenge for daffodil growers. The Gulf Coast climate in particular is difficult because there is little in the way of a cold season, the soil tends to be alkaline, and the summers can be extremely hot. None of these conditions is conducive to *Narcissus* culture. It can be done, however, by taking all the precautions given for other southern climates in addition to amending the often compacted alkaline soils with gypsum and lots of well-decomposed organic matter. The more northern reaches of the south-central area should be fine for daffodil culture with the possible problem of there being an abbreviated spring. Deal with that short season by purchasing early- and late-blooming cultivars and by pre-cooling your bulbs for 6–8 weeks before planting.

Pacific Northwest, Western Canada, and Central-Pacific

Northern California and the Pacific Northwest, including northwestern Canada, are almost ideal areas for growing daffodils due to the abundant spring rainfall, dry summers, and a long, cool growing season. These climatic variables are surpassed only in Holland, where the soil is almost pure beach sand and the water table is controlled below the bulbs. Almost every type of daffodil will thrive in such a moderate climate. People and machinery might rust in the dampness, but daffodils and other plants luxuriate and grow to perfection.

Southwest

As in other warm climate regions, plant your bulbs late (December or January) and water them well to assure root growth. If your soil is heavy, add perlite and gypsum to lighten the texture. Avoid choosing cultivars from divisions 1 through 4 and from division 9 as these tend to be unreliable in warmer climates. Plant in partial shade and insert other types of plants as companions to keep the bulbs cool in summer. If you've never planted daffodils before in this region, it's best to start with jonquillas and tazettas whose ancestors sprang up in warmer climates. If those prove successful, as they probably will, experiment with others from divisions 5 and 6 depending on your particular microclimate. You may want to pre-cool your bulbs for six to eight weeks before planting. Mulch your beds with a light-colored mulch so as to reflect the intense heat from the summer sun away from the soil.

Perennialized daffodils are the first flowers to appear in this three-season meadow in an orchard in Lake Forest, IL.

IV. Naturalized and Perennialized Daffodils

"Naturalized" is a term that's often used in reference to daffodil plantings but is not always clearly defined. Truly naturalized daffodils are those original species *Narcissus* that persist in the wild in Europe and other countries, including those daffodils brought to North America by the first colonists that then escaped to flourish in the wild.

In various parts of the southeastern States there are truly naturalized colonies of species *Narcissus*. Here in Virginia and in the Carolinas we find several variants of *N. pseudonarcissus*. They go by the names of "Lent Lily," "Early Virginia," or "Trumpet Major." *Narcissus bulbocodium* successfully naturalized itself on our farm in Virginia in the rough grass of the lawn and in a thick patch under a grove of mature pines. In a yard in Tyner, North Carolina, we noticed a profusion of *N. bulbocodium* as well as an extensive stand of *N. jonquilla*. *N. ×odorus*, the wild hybrid of *N. jonquilla*, has been naturalized for centuries throughout the Southeast. *N. biflorus* frequently blooms in late April or early May around many old houses and homesites. *N. poeticus* var. *recurvus* is a variety now naturalized in the cooler climates of New England, Canada, and the Mid-Atlantic region.

Unlike hybrid daffodils, wild bulbs adapting to non-native climates propagate primarily by seed. Most species *Narcissus* can self-pollinate but are also cross-pollinated by visiting insects looking for the daffodils' sweet nectar. Species *Narcissus* do not accumulate in thick patches from vegetative division as readily as the hybrids do, but rely on seed dispersal.

Hybrids are the kinds of daffodils most of us use in our "naturalistic" plantings. As a rule, hybrids will form large clumps of plants that can appear to be naturalized, but they will not spread to distant locations because few hybrids set seed. As long as a patch of hybrids receives enough sunlight, water, and nutrients, the patch will continue to perennialize; that is, to expand in size by vegetative division and to bloom year after year. Some hybrids, however, must be dug and either divided or added to periodically in order to flourish.

To achieve the naturalized look with hybrid daffodils, you should try to imagine how an original group of species bulbs might have reseeded and spread at your site. Look at the site

(Pages 56-57) *Perennialized daffodil 'Carlton' with* Ranunculus *show off each other's strengths.* (Opposite) *A naturalistic mass planting of daffodils under tall pines does beautifully in a semishade situation.* (Above) N. bulbocodium *var.* conspicuus *naturalizes in the grass by readily reseeding itself.*

from different angles and take into consideration the layout of shrubs and trees. Remember that species plants tend to follow the contours of the landscape and to stay out in full sunlight or at the sunny edge of a patch of woods.

We often find naturalized bulbs in woods that were once open fields or meadows. In those places, the bulbs came first but were overtaken by trees. Bulbs will grow down to the edges of bodies of water provided there's sufficiently good drainage, but most daffodils cannot stand to have what's known as "wet feet," especially in the summer. With these variables in mind, mark off the area in which you want to create a naturalized planting. Mark it with sticks, flags, or with a garden hose encircling the site to guide you in your planting.

Deciding whether to plant hybrids or species bulbs in your

Large groups of about 100 daffodils make a great focal impact in a natural situation at the Edith L. Carrier Arboretum at James Madison University.

"natural" setting depends on what your goals are for your site. There are seldom mixtures of bulb types to be found in truly naturalized plantings because species *Narcissus* do not cross-pollinate in nature as readily as they self-pollinate. More often you'll see a small to large concentration of one bulb type in an area that feathers out to thinner numbers of plants toward the edges. If your goal is to replicate a genuinely naturalized look, then only species plants that truly naturalize themselves should be used. However, don't expect to create a startling visual impact with species *Narcissus*, since most species flowers are small and graceful. If, on the other hand, your aim is for a mass of color in a natural setting that makes a dramatic visual effect, it's best to use the strongest perennial hybrids.

In many books, it's recommended that you take a handful of bulbs, toss them over your shoulder, and plant them where they land. In our opinion, the bulbs fall too far apart to create a focal effect. You end up with a weak planting.

Every year millions of daffodils are sold in mixtures intended for naturalizing. Again, it's our opinion that mixtures weaken the effect of the planting. The bulbs bloom at different times, so there's always a lot of foliage but not a full-flowered look. If there's too much space between each blooming flower sometimes a fresh flower will be coming into bloom right beside one that is dying.

In nature, wildflowers do not bloom in mixtures of this sort. You might find a white daisy, a blue chicory, and a yellow Coreopsis together in the wild, but seldom are you going to come across white, blue, and yellow daises together. In the wild you'll find blocks of different species that meet and mix by feathering or fingering into one another. You can achieve that feathering effect with patches of perennial daffodils and get a lovely natural look with a lot of color.

V. In the Company of Daffs

COMPANION PLANTINGS

A flower bed filled with combinations of plant material (daffodils, hyacinths, other perennials, annuals, ground covers, vegetables, and woody ornamentals) adds stimulating color and shape to your neighborhood and to your life throughout the year. Perhaps you remember the days when the bulb bed, the vegetable garden, and the annual bed were in separate locations? That was certainly a lackluster way to plant, not to mention all the labor of preparing additional beds! Now with a little planning, most flowers can share the same bed.

Since daffodil bulbs are planted deeper than most other plants, it makes sense to plant your daffodils first. After the *Narcissus* bulbs are in, perennials and ground covers can be added right on top of the bulbs. Just as we sometimes dress ourselves in layers, a flower border can be layered as well.

If you live in a zone where it gets extremely cold very quickly, you may want to wait until spring to plant perennials and ground covers over your planted bulbs. You can insert the later materials just as the daffodils emerge. Using a small trowel to dig the hole, we plant annuals around daffodils just as soon as we can in the spring. By the time the bulbs finish blooming, the annuals have begun to flourish and are so colorful that the bulb foliage acts as a linear accent. At this point we add perennials and vegetable seeds to the border to have an interesting and colorful garden at an otherwise in-between time of the year.

Bulbs complete their major growth and food storage during the short period of time before the other plants are fully active, so there is little competition in a shared bed. Daffodils receive an extra benefit from companion plantings because perennials, annuals, and ground covers mask the sometimes unsightly maturing foliage of the bulbs, so you won't be tempted to cut them too soon. Companion plants then use up excess moisture when the bulbs need to dry in the summer and provide shade from the hot summer sun.

(Opposite) *The combination of 'Hillstar' daffodils and 'Beauty Queen' tulips contrasts two pastel colors that work well together.* (Above) *'Honeybird' daffodils and 'Pink Impression' tulips coordinate their bloom time in this companion planting.*

The Daylily-Daffodil Walk at the New York Botanical Garden illustrates how these two plants are ideal bedfellows. The daylilies hide the maturing daffodil foliage and provide sequential color.

Daffodils and daylilies make wonderful flower bedmates. The daffodils bloom early in the spring, then the tall daylily foliage curves down and hides the maturing daffodil foliage besides providing sequential flowering through the summer. But this combination is only one possibility. Tulips at 10", daffodils at 6", Crocus, Muscari, and *Iris reticulata* on top at 3", will give you continuous blooms for about four months. On the shady side of the flower border add hostas as wonderful companions with Alliums. In that same area you might add some *Arum italicum*, Helleborus, and a few ferns. On the sunny side of your border, Asters, Verbena, and Shasta daisies lengthen the blooming season. Lycoris, Sedum ('Autumn Joy'), Siberian iris, Asiatic lilies, and Chrysanthemums extend the blooming season into fall. Adding pansies, johnny-jump-ups, Cleome, and other annuals would round out your border with so much to see you wouldn't know what to look at first!

Most of the plants we've mentioned, bulbs included, will emerge easily through evergreen ground covers, such as *Vinca minor* or ivy, that make a rich backdrop color beneath the spring blooms. If your region has bitterly cold winters with a lot of snow, you may want to add compact, berried, ornamental trees and shrubs near your border to provide interest and color when other plants are dormant. Berry-type ornamentals offer the advantage, too, of attracting birds to your garden.

Charts on the next pages suggest combinations of plant materials to create various effects you might want from your garden. Our own beds and borders have evolved through the years. We've added plants here, seeds there, divided clumps, and expanded areas. When we look across our yard now, there is always something of horticultural interest and almost always something to pick for an arrangement. Your own plantings, even small ones, can do the same for you.

Companion Plants with Similar Blooming Periods

To help you put together plants with similar blooming periods, here is a list of companion planting possibilities (herbaceous as well as woody) for specific bulb types, including early, midseason, and late daffodils.

Companion Plants with Similar Blooming Periods

Bulb Type	Companion Plants
Allium	Rhododendrons, Hostas, Laburnum, Wisteria, Dicentra, Kniphofia
Anemone	Daffodils, *Cornus florida*, tulips. Use in underplantings or at edge of border.
Anemone blanda	Daffodils, tulips, Daphne, Dicentra, lawn grasses. Use in woodland plantings.
Arum italicum	Helleborus, Colchicum, Crocus (fall), Oxalis
Asiatic lilies	Alliums, daylilies, Coreopsis, Triteleia, lawn grasses
Camassia	Siberian iris, Alliums, Digitalis, Tritileia, ferns
Chionodoxa	*Iris reticulata*, Crocus, early daffodils, early tulips, lawn grasses. Use in woodland plantings.
Colchicum	Sweet alyssum, Asters, Verbena, lawn grasses, Crocus (fall), Cyclamens, Crinodonna, Oxalis, Amarcrinum
Crocus species	Lawn grasses, *Iris reticulata*, Galanthus, Chionodoxa, johnny-jump-ups
Crocus vernus	Pansies, lawn grasses, Puschkinia, early daffodils, Lamium
Daffodils (early)	Forsythia, Kaufmanniana tulips, berried shrubs, *Jasminum nudiflorum*
Daffodils (midseason)	*Magnolia stellata* and *M. soulangiana*, early tulips, Prunus, Bellis
Daffodils (late)	*Brunnera*, Spiraea, columbine, *Cornus florida*, tulips, Leucojum
Daffodils (miniature)	Helleborus, *Phlox subulata*, Arabis, Sedums, Ajuga, *Anemone pulsatilla*
Dutch iris	Peonies, Siberian iris, *Allium moly*, Digitalis, Sweet William, roses
Eremurus	Alliums, Dutch iris, hollyhocks, Digitalis
Erythronium	Mertensia, Primula, Hyacinthoides, hardy geraniums. Use in woodland plantings.
Fritillaria (dwarf)	Dwarf daffodils, Erythronium, Tiarella. Use in meadow and woodland plantings.
Fritillaria imperialis	Daffodils, Euphorbia, *Kerria japonica*, *Viburnum carlesii*, tulips
Galanthus	English ivy, *Vinca minor*, Camellia, Cyclamen, *Arum italicum*
Gladiolus (hardy)	Alliums, Polygonum, Chrysanthemums, *Pyrethrum coccineun*
Hermodactylus tuberosa	Iberis, Helleborus
Hyacinthoides (scilla)	Alliums, Camassias, late daffodils, late tulips. Use in woodland plantings.
Hyacinth	Pansies, *Viola tricolor*, daffodils, tulips, Doronicum
Ipheion	Lawn grasses, tulips, daffodils, Anemones. Use in woodland plantings at edges of borders.
Iris (dwarf)	Lawn grasses, Chionodoxa, winter honeysuckle, flowering quince
Leucojum	Late daffodils, midseason tulips, Mahonia, Muscari, Hyacinthoides

Companion Plants with Similar Blooming Periods (continued)

Bulb Type	Companion Plants
Lilium candidum	Dianthus, Bletilla
Lycoris	Santolina, Stachys, Sedum ('Autumn Joy'), Boltonia, Artemisia
Muscari	Daffodils, tulips, white birch, Anemones. Plant at front of borders.
Oriental lilies	Cleome, Phlox, *Verbena bonariensis*, Achillea, Queen Anne's Lace
Ornithogalum nutans	*Hyacinthoïdes hispanica*, *Phlox stolonifera*, Camassia. Use in woodland plantings.
Oxalis	Ajuga, Artemesia. Use in woodland plantings.
Scilla siberica	Lawn grasses, Amelanchier, Galanthus, Lamiastrum. Use in woodland plantings.
Triteleia	Asiatic lilies, Zantedeschia, hardy Gladiolus, Sweet William
Tulips (early)	Iberis, sweet alyssum, Mysotis, Prunus, daffodils, *Anemone blanda*
Tulips (midseason)	Crab apples, Azaleas, wallflowers, pansies, Rhododendrons
Tulips (late)	Fritillaria, late daffodils, Lunaria, English daisies, ribbon grass
Tulips (miniature)	*Anemone blanda*, *Viola tricolor*, Stachys, Doronicum, herbs

Companion Planting to Extend the Blooming Season

Sun-Loving Companion Plants

Here is a list of sun-loving plants to extend the blooming season of spring bulbs and provide needed cover foliage:

Achillea	Globe Amaranth	Rudbeckea
Ageratum	Liatris	Salvia
Aster	Lily	Shasta daisy
Bearded iris	Marigold	Siberian iris
Belameanda	Nicotiana	Stachys
Chrysanthemum	Pansy	Sweet William
Cleome	Penstemon	Vegetables
Coryopsis	Peony	Verbena
Dahlia	Petunia	*Viola tricolor*
Daylily	Poppy	Zantadescia
Dianthus	Queen Anne's	Zinnias
Gaillardia	Lace	

(Opposite) *This typical garden in The Netherlands utilizes companion plantings to yield color and interest throughout the year.* (Above) *'Thalia'* and Muscari armeniacum *are ideal companions with ground covers like lady's-mantle.*

Shade-Tolerant Companion Plants

The following list is of shade-tolerant plants to extend the blooming season of spring bulbs and provide needed cover foliage:

Ajuga	Hosta
Astilbe	Impatiens
Azalea	Laminum
Begonia	Lobelia
Camellia	Mallows
Campanula	Monarda
Coleus	Nandina
Cyclamen	Oxalis
Digitalis	Primula
English ivy	Rhododendron
Ferns	Sedum
Forget-me-not	Shadbush
Helleborus	*Vinca minor*
Holly	

'Birma' emerges through a bed of Bergenia and is nicely displayed in front of a clump of Euphorbia.

(Pages 68-69) *Clumps of the miniature daffodil 'Sun Disc' are nicely shown off against an alder hedge.* (Above) *The miniature 'Minnow' is an excellent daffodil to grow in a pot for a window box or patio planter.*

MINIATURES AND HEIRLOOMS

Miniature Hybrids and Miniature Species

Miniature hybrids and miniature species are that group of *Narcissus* officially recognized by the American Daffodil Society, many of which are 6" tall or under, and whose flower can be 2" in diameter or smaller. The Society compiles and makes available a list of "Approved Miniatures."

These are marvelous little flowers that deserve a place in every garden. Because of their height, they should be placed at the front of the border, in a rock garden, in the niche of a tree's roots, or forced in pots or pans or larger containers. They work well when planted among short ground cover plants such as periwinkle, Ajuga, thyme, Sedums, and Violas.

A few of the miniature species have extremely tiny bulbs, the size of your little fingernail. It is helpful to plant these in strawberry baskets buried in the soil, to avoid losing the diminutive bulbs. Most other miniatures are large enough, at least thumb-sized, to treat as you would a standard bulb. Plant them at a depth equal to three times their height, usually 3"–4" deep. Also, plant enough of them to make a noticeable statement, at least 10 to a group or, even better, 50 to 100 bulbs each about 3" apart.

We find that many miniature daffodils can be forced with a shorter cold period than their larger relatives (see "Forcing: How to Have Blooms out of Season"). Most sources recommend using shorter, stockier types for forcing as they'll look better in pots if they don't grow too tall. Miniature daffodils fit that to a tee. Make sure you get plenty of miniatures for outdoors and for your forcing projects!

Heirloom Daffodils

Heirloom daffodils have come back in vogue. For years, restoration gardens, such as those at Colonial Williamsburg, Monticello, Mt. Vernon, or at Tryon Palace in North Carolina, have been seeking out cultivars and species that were available during specific historical periods. The gardening public is becoming more aware of these efforts. Now many people are restoring period plants to their gardens as part of their restoration of Colonial, Victorian, or early 20th-century homes.

N. 'Canaliculatus' is a miniature species hybrid daffodil that thrives best when planted deep, fertilized well, and given a southern exposure where it will get a summer baking.

Many of these older cultivars have perennialized themselves so well in gardens that plantings made 100 to 200 years ago are still flourishing. Gardeners are recognizing the hardy persistence of these plants and are seeking them out for naturalized plantings (see "Naturalized and Perennialized Daffodils"). You'll find most of these heirloom cultivars included among the divisions listed in "Recommended Daffodils in Commercial Culture."

ADDITIONAL PLANTING SITES

Outdoor Containers

With more of us living in apartments, condominiums, and houses on small plots of land, the opportunity of growing daffodils in outdoor containers becomes an appealing way to have a small but vivid addition to your neighborhood. Patio planters and window boxes are like little gardens in the air.

From zone 7 and southward, plan to establish your large patio planters in the fall, just as though you were going to put in a garden bed. The dimensions of the planter should be at least four square feet. The interior should be insulated with a layer of foam to withstand temperatures lower than 20°F. If you expect lower temperatures or if your planter is smaller than four square feet, wrap the planter in foam after your bulbs have been planted or bury the planter in a leaf or mulch pile until spring.

A window box will almost always require protection dur-

'Cragford' is an excellent choice to grow in a pot. Like the paper-white, it does not require a cold period.

ing the winter because a window box does not contain enough soil volume to protect its bulbs. Plant your bulbs instead in a soil-filled liner that will fit inside your window box. Transfer the liner to the window box after the danger of a hard freeze is past. If you have storage space to accommodate several window-box liners, plant them with sequentially later-blooming bulbs to provide a sequence of bloom at the window.

If you live in climates colder than zones 7 and 8, you might consider planting bulbs in the fall in individual pots (either peat or plastic pots, with dimensions 2" x 2" x 3"). These little pots or cell packs will each hold the roots of one growing bulb (see "Tricking the Flowers" for more on planting procedures with small individual pots). Next, gather all your planted pots into a tray or box and put a little sand or mulch around each bulb to hold it upright. Place the container tray under 8"–10" of leaves or mulch, or dig a trench, line it with newspapers or leaves, place the bulbs at the bottom, and cover them. The mulch pile or trench should be in a shaded location to help keep cool temperatures stabilized. The bulbs will root into their little pots as they go through their cold period.

The next step comes after the danger of a hard freeze (temperatures lower than 25°F) is past. Remove the individual pots from the container tray as needed and arrange them in an attractive display in your window box or planter. It can be fun to assemble plants reaching different heights by combining small pots of ivy, Vinca, and other decorative perennials or annuals to accent the daffodil bulbs. You're creating a kind of picture or live outdoor flower arrangement. (See "Companion Plantings" for suggested plant combinations.)

For best results with planters and window boxes, choose daffodil cultivars that are naturally short and stocky and that have an appealing fragrance (see "Recommended Daffodils in Commercial Culture"). Cultivars whose flowers tend to look upward are more focally effective in outdoor containers than the pendulous, fuchsia-like daffodils. If you choose cultivars having flowering periods from the earliest to the latest bloom,

(Upper) *Miniature daffodils like 'Little Gem' and* Tulipa humilis *are excellent subjects for strawberry pots.* (Lower) *'Bridal Crown' is one of the best bulbs for patio containers because it is short and fragrant.*

you can have continuous daffodils as part of your container plantings.

When a daffodil in the planter or window box begins to fade, pull out the individual bulb unit and replant it in your garden bed, if you have one. Then install a fresh bulb from your container tray, one just about to bloom, and presto, you keep your outdoor arrangement going on and on with a succession of blooms.

Nestled in Tree Roots

One of our favorite outdoor spots for daffodils, especially miniatures, is in the pockets of tree roots beside the trunks. These little spots give the bulbs a wonderful backdrop that shows them off well. They also receive a little extra protection from the wind and weather. The Naturalizing Tool or a narrow trowel are most effective for planting among tree roots.

Most daffodils prefer full sun, but most will tolerate half shade. Care should be taken, however, when you select trees for this purpose. Trees such as maples, beeches, and dogwoods have fibrous and shallow root systems and should be avoided. Under these trees the stiff competition for nutrients and water may prove too difficult for the bulbs. After all your planting work, what you may see is a great crop of green leaves, but no blooms. Even when bulbs are planted amid the roots of more deeply rooted trees, we recommend that the trees be pruned ("raised" or "limbed up") so that sunlight can filter through.

'Garden Princess' and other cyclamineus types will continue to bloom as long as they receive enough sunlight, water, and nutrients. This clump resulted from a few bulbs that multiplied. (Opposite) The daffodil 'Little Witch', Muscari latifolium, *cowslip, and the daffodil 'Hawera' share a niche between the roots of a large tree. Small bulbs show themselves well with a tree as a backdrop.*

Rock Gardens

A rock garden, whether it's a genuine alpine or mountain garden with boulders or a miniature imitation of an alpine garden, lends itself to the use of species, miniature, and dwarf *Narcissus*. Indeed, many species bulbs originate in mountainous regions and so will be at home in your rock garden. A number of jonquillas and tazettas also prefer to grow beside a rock or in the sloping scree where their bulbs will ripen during the warm, dry

'Tahiti' and 'Flower Drift' are amongst the strongest double daffodils that perform well in partial shade.

period. The elevated layout of a rock garden helps to display the small and compact cultivars and emphasizes their fragrance.

A rock garden can take any number of shapes and sizes. In general, though, every rock garden is an elevated bed that must have, like all daffodil beds, excellent drainage and a good water source during the spring growth period. See "Miniature Hybrids and Miniature Species" and "Recommended Daffodils in Commercial Culture" for detailed information on plants suitable for rock gardening.

Woodland Plantings

Planting daffodils in an established stand of woods can be accomplished fairly readily provided you keep a few things in mind. First, the trees must be deep-rooted rather than fibrous-rooted species so they will not create undue competition for the bulbs (see "Nestled in Tree Roots"). Usually, if other plants are growing well beneath the trees, bulbs will flourish, too.

Second, the trees should be spaced sufficiently far apart that bulbs will receive at least half a day of filtered sunlight through the full foliage. Third, the bulbs should be well fertilized every year (see "Fertilizing") and should receive at least ½" of rainfall per week during April and May.

The fourth consideration is that companion plants such as ferns, Epimedians, *Vinca minor*, Helleborus, Ajuga, and a broad array of woodland wildflowers should follow the daffodil bloom to provide sequential color through the rest of the season. We find the Naturalizing Tool the ideal implement for planting under trees as its design is amenable to digging around tree roots (see "Proper Tools").

Daffodils planted at the very edge of a strip of woods where they receive sufficient sunshine can make a very beautiful effect. If possible, bulbs in such shaded areas should be given a little extra fertilizer and water to help them compete.

'Queen of the North' is a cultivar that has been perennialized in this meadow at Wintherthur for nearly 100 years.

Meadow Plantings

Wildflower meadows have become extremely popular in recent years. Unfortunately, though, many consumers purchase a "Meadow in a Can" and then are disappointed when they don't achieve instant color. This has to do in part with our expectation of instant gratification and in part with the vendors who lead customers to believe that a large garden can be planted successfully with little or no time and effort.

There is another way to create a meadow planting that has worked well for us and others. This method involves killing but not tilling the turf, then plugging in bulbs, perennials, grasses, and annuals to achieve a sequentially blooming meadow from spring to fall.

First, kill the turf cover in the late summer, using one or more applications of Roundup. Do not till up the turf as the

'Ceylon' has upfacing flowers, thick substance, long-lasting blooms, and is a great perennializer.

exposed soil will allow germination of new weed seeds. When the grass has turned brown and it's the proper planting time for bulbs, cut slots in the turf to create holes 6"–8" deep for the bulbs (see "Proper Tools"). Insert the bulb and press the turf in place on top of the bulb.

After the bulbs have been planted, it's time to insert the perennials or plugs between the groups of bulbs. Next, the whole area can be seeded with annuals to achieve sequential color for the rest of the year. Sequential planting guarantees color throughout the growing season as well as cover for the maturing foliage of the bulbs.

Meadow plantings can be maintained by spot weeding once a month during the growing season. If some weeds prove persistent, you can selectively destroy them with an application of Roundup. However, wipe on the herbicide rather than spraying it so that you target only the undesirable plants. We find the best method is to put on dishwashing gloves, then cotton gloves on top of those. Dip a cotton glove into a solution of Roundup mixed with a detergent-and-water solution, then proceed to wipe the solution on the unwanted vegetation.

Mass Plantings

One of the most dramatic and attractive uses of daffodils is to create a "river" of daffodils alongside a road through a woods or a field. When in bloom, the flower river seems to flow with the contour of the landscape. The river is wide in some areas, it flows around trees and

shrubs, then narrows in other places and winds around and about as it leads you to its destination.

Groups of 100 to several thousand bulbs will be required to make such a dramatic addition to a landscape. It's best to use the same one cultivar or, if two or more cultivars are used, let one cultivar gradually merge ("finger" or "feather") into the other cultivar in a casual way.

It's also possible to create a formal design or picture using variously colored daffodils having the same blooming period.

A lovely mass planting of daffodils makes a showy river at Chanticleer in Pennsylvania.

A river of Muscari armeniacum *is edged with 'Geranium' daffodils and 'Red Emperor' tulips looking like beautiful rocks on the banks of a river.*

We once visited a zoo where a large outline of the United States had been grown on a hillside with daffodils; each state was filled in with a different cultivar.

We have also seen geometric patterns of daffodils, in symmetrical and asymmetrical designs. Whatever your idea for a mass planting, keep in mind that daffodils are one of the most cost-effective of all perennials and certainly one of the most dramatic when assembled in large groups.

Planting in Grass

Seeing areas in England where daffodils have been planted in the grass is a charming experience. However, planting daffodils in lawn grass is generally not a good idea in most parts of the United States or in Canada. The reason is that most of our turf grasses, unlike English grasses, mature quickly. When our weather warms up, our grass jumps up and becomes unsightly to those accustomed to manicured lawns. Out come the lawn mowers and, unfortunately, the daffodil foliage gets cut before it has a chance to mature. In general, daffodil foliage needs to be left to grow for at least 8–10 weeks after the blooming period in order to produce enough sugars to bloom the next spring.

We have several options. The first is to plant bulbs in the grass at the far edge of the lawn and allow that section to grow up in rough grass until around the first of June. The second option is to use one of the approved growth retardants to keep the grass from maturing until the bulb foliage has matured. Check with your USDA county extension agent for recommendations of growth retardants for your area as well as methods of application.

Another option for grassy areas is to lay out a meadow (see "Meadow Plantings" above). One bonus from the meadow method is that you have one less section of lawn to mow. We dislike mowing grass, but love to weed and groom our meadow beds.

Community Gardens

Community gardening is something we're beginning to see more and more of around the country. A number of our customers are community volunteers who are beautifying their streets, parks, and public areas with bulb borders and gardens. Their efforts and monies seem to accomplish a lot more than tax dollars spent for the same purpose.

Here in Gloucester county a local resident, Dorothy Parker, sparked the idea of beautifying what was then an ugly traffic triangle. She raised a few dollars for soil-improvement materials, the Daffodil Mart donated tractor time to till in the amendments, and we donated bulbs for the first season. That was only the beginning! Mrs. Parker galvanized the neighborhood's residents to donate other plants from their gardens. Landscape timbers were also donated and now this little garden triangle is lovely all year long, a bright spot for the hundreds of people who drive past it every day.

Now we are seeing other areas in Gloucester being adopted by residents and made more beautiful. One incidental benefit is that these areas are no longer on the maintenance list of areas the state highway department has to mow. We're sure that enthusiasm and energy from one person can make a difference anywhere. Mrs. Parker proves it!

'Flower Record' is planted in the grass of a churchyard that is not mown until the daffodil foliage has matured.

VI. Forcing: How to Have Blooms Out of Season

TRICKING THE FLOWERS

The gentle art of forcing daffodils (or tricking the flowers to bloom earlier than normal) is usually easier with cultivars that normally bloom early. With a little planning you can have daffodils in bloom from Halloween through Easter, in large numbers or just a few in single pots.

The first step is to select suitable cultivars (see "Recommended Daffodils in Commercial Culture"). Purchase them in September or ask for September delivery from your supplier if you want to have forced blooms by early January and February. It's helpful to let your supplier know that the bulbs you're ordering so early are meant for forcing. Most suppliers try hard to help you be successful gardeners by delivering your bulbs at the proper time for garden planting in your area. If normal planting time in your zone is October 30th and you ask for September 15th delivery … well, they might not understand if you don't tell them why!

Most daffodil cultivars require a minimum of 14–16 weeks of constant cold below a certain temperature, a "cold period," in order to trigger the flowering process. What you're doing when you force a bulb is providing a cold period to make the bulb go into its vernalization, or bud formation phase. Some cultivars will take less than the full 16 weeks to complete the rooting and bud formation process. Until specific trials are done, it remains a trial-and-error process to guess the exact length of cold period needed by each variety. As a rule most miniatures, tazettas, and cyclamineus cultivars do well with a somewhat shorter period.

Keeping the total cold period in mind, there are several ways to go about achieving early blooms. You can pot the bulbs immediately if you have a rooting room or a large refrigerator in which the temperature can be held below 60°F for six to eight weeks while the bulbs are rooting, then at 35°–45°F for six to eight weeks longer.

If you don't have access to a rooting room or large refrigerator, you can store your bulbs, unpotted and dry, in a breathable bag in the hydrator of an ordinary refrigerator for the first six-to-eight-week period. Longer than eight weeks

(Opposite) *Strong-stemmed 'Jerusalem' is the largest paper-white.* (Above) *Daffodil bulbs like 'Jenny' can be grown in a broad range of attractive containers.*

for this first stage of cooling will be of little value to forcing the plant; in fact, it will be only a holding time.

When the soil temperature outdoors has fallen to about 60°F (at a depth of 6"–8"), pot the refrigerated bulbs. Place the bulbs so they are just touching: usually five standard-sized bulbs to a 6" pot, nine bulbs to a 12" pot. These containers should then be placed outdoors, thickly covered under a mulch pile, for another six to eight weeks to complete the rooting process.

We find the best potting-soil medium to be a fairly coarse-textured growing mix instead of a fine-textured seedling mix. Mixes used by commercial growers often contain peat moss, finely ground pine bark, perlite, and granite sand. Coarse mixes allow easy penetration and traction for the roots as well as support for the roots and, most importantly, good drainage. Brand names of suitable potting media currently available include "Metro Mix," "Jiffy Mix," and "Pro Mix."

After planting, water the potted bulbs and medium thoroughly. Do not water again until the top of the potting soil feels dry. Usually one or two light waterings are sufficient during this part of the rooting and cooling period.

Another type of container for forcing bulbs is the cell pack. These offer many exciting alternatives to conventional pot or pan methods. The empty cells, generally 1 ½" to 2 ½" square and about 3" deep, are made of plastic or peat. About 35 of the 2" cells will fit into a standard nursery tray.

The cells should be filled full and level with potting mix. One bulb should then be perched on top of the potting mix in one cell so that the cell will contain only roots from one growing bulb. To hold the bulbs in place while they root, sand, bark, or more potting soil may be propped around the base of the bulbs. The cells should then be stored through the usual cold period.

One of several advantages to forcing with cell packs is that because each bulb has its own growing space, roots from adjacent bulbs do not intertwine. You also have the option of removing a few bulbs and forcing only as many as you wish for a particular blooming time. A varied group can be

selected to create an arrangement of different heights and colors in a decorative container for a long-lasting live flower arrangement.

Another advantage to forcing with cell packs is the flexibility it allows you to select only those bulbs that have reached a certain stage of development. This as-sures you of a more uniform display of forced flowers and it provides a later crop of replacements from bulbs that didn't mature as rapidly as the first. Given a tray of 35 bulbs planted at the same time, there will be at least a week or two be-tween the earliest and latest blooms.

Bulbs forced in cell packs can be easily replanted outdoors after the danger of a hard freeze is past, giving you an instant spring garden or instant color in a window box or patio planter (see "Outdoor Containers").

If the goal of your forcing scheme is a flower show or an indoor display scheduled for a particular date, it's a good idea to start with many more bulbs than you plan on exhibiting. The rule of thumb used by the forcing industry is to start with twice as many bulbs as you think you'll need for the display.

Regardless of the method you use for the cold period of forcing, once roots begin emerging from the bottom of the pot it's time to bring them into the house or greenhouse. This is the phase of forcing when applied bottom heat and grow lights are the most important factors to promote quick emer-gence of blooms.

Ideally the temperature of the planted pots should be about 70°F, with the ambient temperature of the greenhouse or room about 50° to 60°F. Heat mats or heat tapes are the most efficient means of providing constant bottom heat. "Salton" food warmer trays and other such warming devices can be pressed into service. The top of a household refrigera-tor, too, is generally a constant 70°F or more.

Your bulbs need to have the maximum amount of avail-able daylight to achieve normal height and develop maximum

'Hawera' is one of the smallest minia-ture daffodils and also one of the most versatile.

color. Supplemental daylight can be provided by grow lights or fluorescent lights for a few extra hours in the evening. Lack of sufficient light will result in leggy stems that aren't strong enough to hold up the blossoms.

Once the flower buds begin to emerge, it is important to give the pots more attention. Water them several times a week as the tops of the pots will dry out more quickly now. But don't keep the pots waterlogged as this may lead to root rot. A bit of granular charcoal added to the potting mix can help keep the soil free from mold and fungus.

Fertilizing is of little benefit at this point unless the bulbs are intended for planting outdoors after the frost date. If that's your plan, keep the pots in maximum daylight, water them well, and fertilize them with a water-soluble formula high in phosphorus, potash, and trace elements. Adding calcium nitrate several weeks before bloom will help to strengthen the stems.

FORCING IN INDOOR CONTAINERS

Containers for indoor forcing can range from the traditional flower pot or bulb pan to an urn or basket or wooden planter. Just about any interesting container can be put to use: a chafing dish, fishbowl, canister, wooden box, hollow log, battery jar, compote dish, pitcher, bedpan, old shoe, or a traditional clay pot or planter.

Start by selecting the bulbs with a plan in mind for when you'd like them to bloom. For the easiest indoor forcing, certain groups of daffodils give the best results. One such group is the winter-blooming, tender bulbs from climates that do not have a cold period. These include the tazettas called "paper whites" and their kin. There are about ten varieties of these bulbs (see "Recommended Daffodils in Commercial Culture"), usually available from suppliers between September and Christmas.

Store the tazettas in a warm spot such as on top of your refrigerator, not inside your refrigerator as the cold may inhibit or abort the bloom. The 'Ziva' paper-white cultivar can be started early and be in bloom by Halloween; other paper-

whites will bloom from Thanksgiving until Easter. If you start these bulbs at two-week intervals you'll have flowers all winter and spring.

To pot up your tazettas for forcing: use pots three-quarters filled with a coarse-textured potting mix (made of two parts peat moss, two parts ground pine bark, one part perlite, and one part sharp builders sand). There are several suitable commercial formulas, including "Fafard Mix #4," "Metro Mix Growing Medium #510," or "Pro-Mix BX-Growing Medium." Place the bulbs side by side in the pot, then fill around the bulbs with pebbles to hold the bulbs in place.

A version of this potting method is to fill in around the bulbs with more potting soil and plant rye seed (a grassy annual), so that you'll have a nice carpet of green in the pot by the time the tazettas bloom.

Another method is to grow your tazettas in individual small pots according to procedures described in "Outdoor Containers." However, you will not be making use of an outdoor trench or mulch pile as tazettas are not hardy for most areas. Once the tazettas have emerged, choose whatever decorative container you'd like to use, line it with plastic if it's not waterproof, and set up your arrangement. You might choose paper-whites of several sizes and colors to bloom simultaneously, adding some foliage plants for accent. You might do almost anything. Give your imagination free rein and try a lot of combinations.

Another reliable group of daffodils good for indoor forcing are the early-blooming bulbs that require only a short cold period of 8–10 weeks. Review "Tricking the Flowers" for procedures for handling these bulbs. If you choose to use the individual-pot method, which we recommend, you'll have more flexibility.

VII. Hybridizing: Making New Daffodils

For us, hybridizing (or breeding) new cultivars has been one of the most exciting and rewarding parts of growing daffodils. It has also been one of the most time-consuming, involving long waits to see results. It takes five to seven years from the time of planting the seed to seeing the first bloom. But it's worth the wait. And if you hybridize every year, you'll always have new surprises each spring after the first bloom, like another Christmas every spring!

The subject of hybridizing can be complex, with genetic studies and chromosome counts to consider, elaborate precautions against insect pollinization to be taken, and volumes of records to be kept. However, as our friend Grant Mitsch once wrote to us, "Brent, you just need to remember that you are only a bee in the hands of the Lord. It is you who spreads the pollen and it is He who creates so many wonderful hybrids."

We have taken his advice and have tried to pollinate a large number of flowers in each of the crosses we make. Our general goal is to breed small, fragrant flowers for the small home garden spaces of the future and to make crosses that will yield significantly different and better hybrids than the 25,000 already introduced.

Daffodil flowers have both male and female organs of procreation. So we go out into our fields and gardens with a vase of cultivars we've selected to be the "fathers," whose pollen is fresh and viable, from flowers that have opened no more than a couple of days before. We approach a cultivar we think might make a viable "mother" to be the seed parent and then we pollinate the flowers by hand by daubing pollen from the anther of the father to the stigma at the end of the pistil of the mother.

Good characteristics we look for in both parents include sunproof color, strong stem, good substance, unusual color, long-lasting flowers, and good growth habits. We might mate two with similar characteristics to try to strengthen those, or

(Opposite) *A blue ribbon seedling,* 'Katie Heath' ('Accent' × N. triandrus albus), *combines the color of the large-cupped 'Accent' with the characteristics of the daffodil species* triandrus albus. (Upper) *'Accent,' the seed parent or "mother" of this seedling.* (Lower) N. triandrus albus, *the pollen parent or "father" of this seedling.*

we might mate two with different characteristics in the hope of introducing a new combination.

We try to work consistently from one generation of seedlings to the next, a practice known as line breeding, in order to strengthen the characteristics we're looking for. The majority of our crosses involve small, miniature, or species *Narcissus* crossed with larger, stronger standards with the hope of creating intermediate to miniature daffodils having strength and fragrance.

One day, though, we deviated from our line breeding and made a cross that was considered by the man of our team to be "a ridiculous cross that will only make a freak!" However, as it turned out, that new seedling (we haven't named it yet) became the first in a line of lovely, multiflowered, split-corona daffodils that have won awards in flower shows. Since then we've tried to be more open-minded in our breeding approach.

If you'd like to try your hand at hybridizing, we recommend you select your favorite daffodil division, or two divisions, and work with them. Do a little research through the daffodil societies to see whether your two prospects share a history as successful parents or whether either is reputed to be sterile. Cross a lot of flowers, be patient while they grow, and enjoy them when they bloom.

The authors breed new cultivars of daffodils. (Opposite) 'Stratosphere' is one of the tallest and finest American-bred jonquilla hybrids.

VIII. Flower Arranging, Shows, and Exhibitions

ARRANGING DAFFODILS

Narcissus lends itself wonderfully to the decorative crafts associated with flower arranging. Picked daffodils can be used in a myriad of ways, from mixed arrangements and bouquets to a simple group of daffodils alone. They can be arranged in water or in Oasis®. Some daffodils can even be dried and used for a while in dried arrangements.

If you're interested in arranging daffodils, be sure to pick your selected flowers when they're just opening. Also, pick your flowers by hand rather than cutting them. That way the stems will be solid at the bottom and able to hold more water in the hollow center tube (see "Showing Daffodils" below for more information on hand picking).

Before arranging daffodils with other flowers, condition your picked flowers in tepid water for a couple of hours to harden them off. Remember that the juice of daffodils is poisonous and will shorten the vase life of other flowers if the daffodils aren't conditioned separately for a period of time. The floral preservative "Silver-Thiosulfate" is the only additive we know of that enhances the vase life of daffodils.

Once conditioned, the flowers can be easily arranged in Oasis® in many different ways and shapes. Some daffodil stems are stiff enough to push into the Oasis® while others will stand firmly after a pencil has been inserted into the Oasis® to make a hole. With the use of Oasis®, you can achieve tall spires of flowers that are striking and unusual. Or you can fill a shallow bowl with a block of it and cut the daffodil stems short to create a graduated mound of flowers. Some daffodil stems will take a curved shape if they're gently rolled across the edge of a table as you might do to curl a ribbon. You can then have daffodils cascading in different curves from the top of your arrangement.

With their bright and their pastel colors, daffodils combine and contrast well with many flowers that bloom at the same time. They are also beautifully displayed against a backdrop of evergreens. Let your imagination go wild. Casual arrangements might not win you blue ribbons at a flower show, but

(Opposite) *Individual forced bulbs of 'Thalia,' 'Pink Pride,' and 'Christmas Marvel' are arranged creatively with blue pansies.* (Above) Oasis® *is a versatile medium in which to arrange daffodils. It allows arrangements of varying shapes, sizes, forms, and heights.*

they'll win you lots of happiness. Take an arrangement to a friend who needs a lift. Join a local garden club to learn more about putting together prize-winning arrangements if that's something you'd like to try. We're sure it can be a lot of fun; we just haven't gotten around to that yet!

SHOWING DAFFODILS

The Competitive Garden Sport

Can you imagine a spectator sport in which contestants use peaceful daffodil flowers to compete against each other in the judging circle? This has become quite an active sporting event in recent years. Thirty-seven shows sponsored by the American Daffodil Society are held all over the United States, along with a score of other shows on a somewhat different or smaller scale.

Quite a lot of planning and effort go into putting a daffodil show together. The local committees are usually from a daffodil society in that area, but the shows draw members from societies in several states or surrounding areas. The committees always welcome extra hands to help with the show.

Helping to stage an exhibition is a great way to learn more about daffodils in your region. Be sure to visit one of the shows in your area. Most members are generous with their knowledge and even with their surplus bulbs. Don't be put off by the occasional "instant expert" who, after just a few years of growing, is critical of what most other growers are doing. There are plenty of down-to-earth people who are helpful to newcomers, so seek them out. Some shows include "Beginners" or "Novice" classes and those are usually thriving. See "Dates and Places of American Shows" to see what's going on in your part of the country.

Once you've grown a few daffodils and visited a few shows, you may be tempted to pick some of your special daffodils to exhibit, too. Here are several thoughts that may help you enjoy your experience and even win some prizes.

Daffodil judges select collections for blue ribbons.

The first thing to learn is the difference between the showy garden flowers that look so spectacular in your garden and the show-quality daffodils that have characteristics to win blue ribbons.

Let's take two examples of "showy" and "show." The cultivar 'Unsurpassable' is one of the largest, showiest daffodils now available. It is a beautiful flower. But when we look closely, we see that its form is not uniform or symmetrical. The petals are twisted rather than flat and overlapping, and the trumpet is often uneven. The substance is thick but not smooth. Its color is usually good but the pose is often poor: its head hanging down a bit instead of looking right up at you. The stem and overall size are usually fine if it has been well grown and if it has been carefully picked so as to maximize stem length.

So the 'Unsurpassable' fails on several areas of form, substance, and pose, which generally keeps it from winning a prize in a show. Nevertheless it remains an excellent choice for a showy garden flower.

On the other hand, 'Arctic Gold' is a cultivar that often contends for a blue ribbon. Its flowers are almost always show quality. It can be relied on for nearly perfect form, thick substance, smooth texture, upright military-type pose, and a size reflecting its good growth habit. In addition to being an excellent show flower it is also a superb garden plant.

Now that we have an idea of what to look for in a show flower, we need to begin to make selections. To begin your wish list, first attend a show and jot down the ribbon winners that appeal to you. Next, order daffodil catalogs (see "Sources for Bulbs") and select those cultivars listed as show flowers or ribbon winners. Third, scan The American Daffodil Society's *Daffodil Journal* for its popularity polls and show reports. These indicate which cultivars consistently win.

Sometimes, the newer show flowers can be expensive, eliminating the possibility of purchase for those on a tight budget. Keep in mind that there are plenty of old-timers that are reasonably priced and still win many ribbons. You really don't need a fat bank account to compete.

'Unsurpassable' (upper) *is the showy garden flower, while* 'Arctic Gold' (lower) *is the beautifully formed, blue-ribbon show flower.*

The N. *'Ambergate'* × N. jonquilla *is awarded the best seedling in the show.*

Plant your bulbs keeping in mind the best cultural practices. You may want to install a windbreak or locate your beds where emerging flowers will be protected from the buffeting spring winds. Wind often damages the flowers by making tiny nicks or cuts in the perianth segments.

Another consideration is to locate your plantings in different exposures or microclimates so that you'll have flowers at the peak of their bloom for several different show dates through the season. Also, you might want to put an inconspicuous label beside the bulbs to identify the cultivar. Keep a list of your cultivars or a map of your planting, either in your files or on your computer. That will help you identify the cultivar when you pick it for the show.

When the flowers are emerging, make sure they get at least ½" of water per week, either from natural rainfall or drip irrigation. As the buds prepare to open, keep an eye on them daily and select the finest flowers as they begin to open fully. Some of the best are those left on the stem to develop. If a hard freeze or heavy shower threatens, pick the flowers a bit early and let them mature in a cool place.

Be sure to pick the flowers rather than cutting them. Take care not to cut the daffodil foliage. To pick, run your forefinger down the stem to the point where it and the leaves come out of the ground, then put your thumb on the other side of the stem as if you were holding a pencil. Gently but firmly pull up and snap off all in the same motion. You now have a solid stem with a white bottom. It helps at this time to write the name of the cultivar carefully on the stem with an indelible marker.

Immediately plunge the picked stem into tepid water. Silver-Thiosulfate is thought to be beneficial to the vase life of picked daffodils. Add it according to the directions.

Your flower should be stored in a cool place until it's time to prepare for the show. It is best not to hold a picked flower in storage for more than a few days. A non-frostfree refrigerator is better for storage since a frostfree refrigerator tends to dry out the blooms. Light misting is helpful, but avoid leaving water drops as these may stain the flower.

Begin preparing your blooms for a show by comparing your picked candidates carefully. Select the youngest among the mature flowers, the one that has the least number of faults or faults that can be corrected. If the flower has any dirt or foreign matter on it, clean it with a cotton swab or a small paintbrush. If the dirt or stain is persistent, dip the cotton swab in milk and gently wash the area. Avoid too much pressure since that can bruise the flower.

If these don't work, you might try what a friend of mine does. I once noticed her kissing a flower, or so I thought. When I laughed, she haughtily informed me that she wasn't kissing the flower at all, she was just licking off a piece of dirt! It worked, too.

Once the flower is clean, check its posture. If the head nods, massage the neck of the flower gently but firmly with upward strokes. If the trumpet is cocked too high, use the reverse procedure. If the petals and sepals are not in line with the stem, gently twist the flower until the bottom petals and top sepal are symmetrical with the stem. If some of the petals or sepals do not lie flat on the same plane as the rest, gently but firmly massage them back into place.

If during all this you become a little heavy-handed and the flower comes off in your hand, do not despair. This has happened to all of us and it's why you have backup flowers!

All this might seem complicated, but it isn't, really. Remember this is just for fun, even though some people get serious and competitive about it. If you enjoy working with flowers these preparations will come naturally with just a little practice.

The night before and the morning of the show, there will be experienced show people around the set-up area who'll be happy to help you fill out the entry cards and place your flowers in the proper class. Having with you a printed list of the cultivars in your garden can be helpful for your flower's identification. If you're still not sure if its identity, scan for similar flowers that have been entered on the bench.

Their hollow stems that retain water allow picked daffodils to be shipped out of water for several days.

Enter your flowers, find something to do for a few hours while the judges are making their decisions, and then, when the show opens, rush back in to see how your babies have fared. If they didn't win in the class you entered, look closely at the winning entrants to learn why they were judged superior. That way you'll know better what to look for from your garden. Then at the next show, when you return to the flower you entered to find that it won a ribbon, you'll be hooked: you'll be another daffodil junkie!

Exhibition Beds and Daffodil Cemeteries

For those who like to try growing every new bulb that arrives on the market, the specialized method of making an exhibition bed is called the "Cemetery Plot." We sometimes think it must have been devised by a group of engineers and priests who felt that all bulbs should be laid to rest in rectangular order. Usually these beds are front-yard exhibitions, with bulbs in precise rows having a white label like a headstone at each cultivar.

Many blue ribbon flowers have been picked from this extensive daffodil cemetery located near the street to let passersby enjoy the beauty of the individual flowers.

There are advantages to the cemetery layout if you're intent on growing flowers for show competition, but in our opinion it isn't a pretty way to grow a pretty flower. A large percentage of American Daffodil Society (ADS) members grow their bulbs by this method and swear by it or will swear at you if you dare to suggest another way. A smaller percentage of ADS members, ourselves among them, include our show bulbs as part of mixed borders along with many other compatible plants. The cemetery system works, but why not have the best of both worlds and include your blue-ribbon flowers in your regular border?

Several factors we consider important for those who wish to make exhibition beds are these:

a) keep your beds mulched to help keep the flowers clean;

b) select an area with a good windbreak to keep the flowers unbroken and unblemished;

c) maintain proper nutrient and moisture levels in the soil;

d) grow enough bulbs of each cultivar to provide a good selection;

e) label each cultivar with a durable marker, such as the vinyl markers that do not get brittle in sunlight. With an indelible marker write the name of the cultivar, including division and color code, on the label. It's best to face the label away from the sun or bury the written part so that it will not fade. Relabel every year or two;

f) make a map of the planted area in case your labels get moved;

g) pick your flowers at optimum development;

h) when you dig and divide your bulbs (every three to five years to keep the blooms at optimum size), share some of your increase with others. Try to get someone else interested in bulb flowers.

Longwood Gardens in Pennsylvania stages the ultimate daffodil show in the Fern Room.

Dates and Places of American Shows

Here's a list of annual shows sponsored by the American Daffodil Society:

Dates and Places of American Shows

Date	Location
Early March	Northern California Daffodil Society at Alden Lane Nursery, Livermore, CA
Early March	Central Mississippi Daffodil Society, Mississippi College, Clinton, MS
Mid-March	Texas Daffodil Society, Dallas Arboretum, Dallas, TX
Mid-March	Fortuna Garden Club, River Lodge Conference Center, Fortuna, CA
Mid-March	Northern California Daffodil Society, Kautz Ironstone Vineyard, Murphys, CA
Mid-March	Georgia Daffodil Society, Atlanta Botanic Gardens, Atlanta, GA
Late March	Oregon Daffodil Society, Amity Grade School, Amity, OR
Late March	Arkansas Daffodil Society, Hendrix College, Conway, AR
Late March	Garden Study Club of Hernando, First Regional Library, Hernando, MS
Late March	East Tennessee Daffodil Society, University of Tennessee Agriculture Campus, Knoxville, TN
Late March	Garden Club of Virginia, location changes yearly, VA

Dates and Places of American Shows (continued)

Date	Location
Late March	Oregon Daffodil Society, Oregon Garden, Silverton, OR
Late March	Greater St. Louis Daffodil Society, Missouri Botanical Garden, St. Louis, MO
Late March	Middle Tennessee Daffodil Society, Cheekwood Botanic Gardens, Nashville, TN
Late March	North Carolina Daffodil Society, North Carolina Botanical Garden, Chapel Hill, NC
Late March	Virginia Daffodil Society, Lewis Ginter Botanical Garden, Richmond, VA
Early April	Upperville Garden Club, Trinity Parish House, Upperville, VA
Early April	Kentucky Daffodil Society, Louisville, KY
Early April	Wichita Daffodil Society, Botanica, Wichita, KS
Early April	Garden Club of Gloucester, Page Middle School, Gloucester, VA
Early April	Somerset County Garden Club, Peninsula Bank, Princess Anne, MD
Mid-April	Daffodil Growers South, Leota Barn, Scottsburg, IN
Mid-April	Shenandoah-Potomac District of West Virginia Garden Clubs, Zion Episcopal Church, Charles Town, WV
Mid-April	Federated Garden Clubs of Maryland, London Town Public House, Edgewater, MD
Mid-April	Oregon Daffodil Society, Washington County Fairgrounds, Hillsboro, OR
Mid-April	Southwest Ohio Daffodil Society, Cincinnati Zoo and Botanical Gardens; (alternates between Cincinnati and Dayton, at the Wegerzyn Center).
Mid-April	Washington Daffodil Society, Brookside Gardens, Wheaton, MD
Mid-late April	Adena Daffodil Society, Veterans' Medical Center, Chillicothe, OH
Mid-late April	Indiana Daffodil Society, Meridian Street United Methodist Church, Indianapolis, IN
Mid-late April	Maryland Daffodil Society, Church of the Redeemer, Baltimore, MD
Mid-late April	New Jersey Daffodil Society, Frelinghuysen Arboretum, Morristown, NJ
Mid-late April	Central Washington Daffodil Club, Yakima Area Arboretum; Yakima, WA
Mid-late April	Central Ohio Daffodil Society, Franklin Park Conservatory, Columbus, OH
Mid-late April	Daffodil and Hosta Society of Western Pennsylvania, Galleria Mall, Pittsburgh, PA
Mid-late April	Chambersburg Garden Club and Tuscarora Daffodil Group, First Lutheran Church, Chambersburg, PA
Mid-late April	Delaware Valley Daffodil Society, Longwood Gardens, Kennett Square, PA
Mid-late April	The Garden Club of Shelter Island, St. Mary's Parish Hall, Shelter Island, NY
Mid-late April	Seven State Daffodil Society, Tower Hill Botanic Garden, West Boylston, MA

DAFFODIL GARDENS ON DISPLAY

Following is a list of public areas throughout the United States featuring interesting displays of daffodil plantings:

Agecroft. Richmond VA
American Horticultural Society. Alexandria VA
Atlanta Botanical Garden. Atlanta GA
Barnsley Gardens. Adairsville GA
Bartlett Arboretum. Stamford CT
Berkshire Botanical Garden. Stockbridge MA
Birmingham Botanical Garden. Birmingham AL
Bob Jones University. Greenville SC
Botanica. Wichita KS
Brookgreen Gardens. Murrells Inlet SC
Brooklyn Botanic Garden. Brooklyn NY
Brookside Gardens. Wheaton MD
Callaway Gardens. Pine Mountain GA
Chadwick Arboretum. Columbus OH
Chanticleer. Wayne PA
Cheekwood Botanical Garden. Nashville TN
Chicago Botanic Gardens. Chicago IL
Cincinnati Civic Garden Center. Cincinnati OH
Cincinnati Zoo and Botanic Garden. Cincinnati OH
Cleveland Botanical Garden. Cleveland OH
Cleveland Metroparks. Cleveland OH
College of William and Mary. Williamsburg VA
Colonial Williamsburg. Williamsburg VA
Columbus Zoo. Powell OH
Des Moines Botanical Center. Des Moines IA
Filoli Gardens. Woodside CA
Frelinghuysen Arboretum. Morristown NJ
Gardenview Horticultural Park. Strongville OH
George W. Heath Memorial Garden. Gloucester VA
Gloucester County Parks and Recreation. Gloucester VA
Golden Eagle Golf Course. Williamsburg VA
Hampton Roads Agricultural Experiment Station.
    Virginia Beach VA
Harrisburg Area Community College. Harrisburg PA

(Upper) *Cheekwood Botanical Garden in Nashville has an extensive daffodil collection.* (Lower) *The Cincinnati Zoo displays the daffodil 'Trevithian' in its lawn. A growth retardant is used to keep the grass from growing while the daffodil foliage matures.*

(Upper) *Longwood Gardens features incredible numbers of perennialized daffodils in the spring.* (Lower) *The Lewis Ginter Botanical Garden in Richmond has one of the most extensive daffodil collections in the country.*

Holden Arboretum. Kirtland OH

Indianapolis Museum of Fine Arts. Indianapolis IN

Inniswood. Columbus OH

James Madison University. Harrisonburg VA

J. Sergeant Reynolds Community College. Goochland VA

Kingwood Center. Mansfield OH

Lewis Ginter Botanical Garden. Richmond VA

Londontown Gardens. Edgewater MD

Longhouse Foundation. East Hampton NY

Longwood Gardens. Kennett Square PA

Masonic Homes. Elizabethtown PA

Maymont. Richmond VA

McCrellis Garden. Bethesda MD

Milliken Corporation. Spartenburg SC

Minnesota Landscape Arbor. Chanhassen MN

Missouri Botanical Gardens. St. Louis MO

Monticello. Charlottesville VA

Morris Arboretum. Philadelphia PA

Mount Vernon. Mount Vernon VA

National Arboretum. Washington DC

New York Botanical Garden. Bronx NY

Niche Gardens. Chapel Hill NC

Norfolk Botanical Garden. Norfolk VA

North Carolina Arboretum. Asheville NC
North Carolina State University Arboretum.
   Raleigh NC
Old Westbury Gardens. Old Westbury NY
Pennsylvania Horticultural Society. Philadelphia PA
Pennsylvania State University. University Park PA
Pepsico Statuary Gardens. Purchase NY
Pittsburg Civic Garden Center. Pittsburg PA
Princeton University. Princeton NJ
Reeves-Reed Arboretum. Summit NJ
Riverbanks Zoo. Columbia SC
Rockefeller Center. New York City NY
Salisbury State University. Salisbury MD
Sandhills Community College. Southern Pines NC
San Diego Zoo and Botanic Garden. San Diego CA
Sixth Street Market. Richmond VA
Skylands Association. Ringwood NJ
Somerset County Parks. Somerset NJ
Southern Living Gardens. Birmingham AL
Smithsonian Institution. Washington DC
Sunset Gardens. Menlo Park CA
Tower Hill Botanic Garden. Boyleston MA
Tryon Palace. New Bern NC
University of Southern California Botanic Garden.
   Irvine CA
University of Georgia. Athens GA
University of Nebraska. Lincoln NE
Virginia Museum of Fine Arts. Richmond VA
VPI Horticulture Garden. Blacksburg VA
Washington Park Arboretum. Seattle WA
University of Richmond. Richmond VA
University of Virginia. Charlottesville VA
Vines Botanical Gardens. Logonville GA
Virginia House. Richmond VA
Washington Park Zoo. Portland OR
Whetstone Garden. Columbus OH
William Paca Gardens. Annapolis MD
Winterthur. Winterthur DE

(Upper) *The McCrellis Garden is an excellent example of a woodland azalea/rhododendron/daffodil companion planting.* (Middle) *The New York Botanical Garden boasts the largest collection of daffodils in commerce. Shown here is the Liason Collection.* (Lower) *The N.C. State University Arboretum, a garden for and by the students, has a collection of several hundred cultivars.* (Pages 104-105) *The pink-cupped daffodil 'Rosy Wonder' and the tulip 'Orange Emperor' are surprisingly complementary.*

IX. Recommended Daffodils in Commercial Culture

In the list below, we describe daffodil cultivars as they grow here in Virginia. Keep in mind that rainfall, sunlight, soil, wind, and general climatic conditions can all affect the time of bloom, flower height, and intensity of flower color.

Cultivars are listed in alphabetical order under the official daffodil divisions. To indicate blooming times we use the terms "early," "midseason," and "late," because gardens in Maine, Minnesota, or Texas will all have their own particular blooming periods. "Midseason" means the peak of the season, when the greatest number of daffodils are in bloom. Dates cited in the descriptions indicate when the cultivar was introduced.

DIVISION I:
TRUMPET DAFFODILS

Overall characteristics: There is one flower to a stem. The trumpet or corona is as long or longer than the perianth segments. Most trumpets perform better in Canada and in the midwestern and northern states than in the Deep South. These cultivars are best as bedding plants, to create a focal impact. Excellent cultivars in Division I:

'**Arctic Gold**' Goldenrod yellow. Show flower with excellent, waxy, smooth substance. Good form and posture. All-purpose, long-lasting flower. Height 12"–16". Midseason bloomer.

'**Beersheba**' Opens creamy yellow, turns clear white by maturity. Long, narrow trumpet. Long-term, excellent perennial. Heirloom, 1926. Height 14"–16". Early midseason bloomer.

'**Bravoure**' White petals with a distinctive yellow trumpet that is long and narrow. Extremely large, strong, floriferous. Excellent show flower. Long-lasting perennial. Height 18"–24". Midseason to late bloomer.

'**Chinese Coral**' Rounded, creamy white petals. Rich salmon, straight trumpet that flares and scallops at the end. Delicate looking, but strong. Height 12"–16". Midseason bloomer.

'**Dutch Master**' Most popular yellow trumpet cultivar. Often a substitute for 'King Alfred.' Showy, up-facing trumpet. Can be forced. Height 18"–20". Early midseason bloomer.

'**Empress of Ireland**' Can open with creamy cup, promptly matures to pure white. Overlapping petals, straight cup flared at the end. Best long-term garden white trumpet. Height 18"–20". Midseason bloomer.

'Holland Sensation' White with yellow trumpet. Giant, bold. Showy in landscapes and mass plantings. Height 18"–24". Late midseason bloomer.

'Honeybird' Glowing pastel yellow petals with white cup. Excellent show flower. Long-lasting perennial. American bred. Height 18"–20". Midseason bloomer.

'India' Rich bright-yellow flower with a halo of white. Golden amber trumpet. Enormous, showy cut flower and bedding plant. Height 18"–20". Midseason bloomer.

'King Alfred' type. All yellow trumpet. America's favorite daffodil. Usually 'Dutch Master' or 'Golden Harvest' cultivars are substituted. Height 16"–18". Early bloomer.

'Las Vegas' Creamy white petals, canary yellow trumpet. Strong, giant, showy grower. An eye-catching bedding plant. Height 18"–20". Midseason bloomer.

'Marieke' Golden yellow trumpet with lots of substance. Improvement on 'Unsurpassable' cultivar. Large, showy. Makes a fine mass display. Can be forced. Height 18"–24". Early midseason bloomer.

'Modoc' All deep yellow. Exceptionally strong grower with fine form. Show flower. American bred. Height 16"–18". Midseason bloomer.

'Mount Hood' White petals with creamy yellow trumpet that matures to white. Moderate grower. Heirloom, 1937. Height 15"–17". Midseason bloomer.

'Pay Day' Yellow petals, somewhat recurved, with halo at base, yellow trumpet. Exquisite for show, great garden plant. Height 14"–16". Early midseason bloomer.

'Pistachio' Soft yellow petals with greenish cast and white halo. White cup with yellow edge. It glows! Height 14"–16". Midseason bloomer.

'Primeur' One of the deepest golden yellow cultivars. One of the latest yellows to bloom. Long-lasting and floriferous. Excellent for bedding. Height 18"–20". Late midseason bloomer.

'Rashee' Ivory white, overlapping perianth. Stovepipe cup slightly flared at tip. Height 14"–16". Early midseason bloomer.

'Rijnveld's Early Sensation' Yellow petals and trumpet. Resembles 'King Alfred' cultivar. The earliest trumpet to bloom: January to February in Virginia. Forces with a short cold period. Height 12"–14". Extremely early bloomer.

'Spellbinder' Greenish, sulfur yellow with trumpet turning white. Striking in landscape plantings. Height 16"–18". Midseason bloomer.

'Topolino' Cream and soft yellow. Dwarf cultivar. Good for rock gardens, pots, and forcing. Height 8"–10". Early midseason bloomer.

'Unsurpassable' Golden yellow. The giant open trumpet is extremely showy. Easy to force. Height 18"–22". Early midseason bloomer.

'Vintage Rose' Flower opens with rich, salmon-pink trumpet. The best pink garden trumpet daffodil we've seen to date. Strong grower. Height 14"–16". Late midseason bloomer.

DIVISION II: LARGE-CUPPED DAFFODILS

Overall characteristics: There is one flower to a stem. The cup or corona is more than one-third but less than equal to the length of the perianth segments. These cultivars are the workhorses of the daffodil world: good for bedding, picking, naturalizing, forcing, and showing. Excellent cultivars in Division II:

'**Accent**' White petals with the best, most intense, sunproof pink cup. Vigorous grower, good naturalizer. Strong substance for show and garden. American bred. Height 14"–16". Midseason bloomer.

'**Ambergate**' Coppery orange suffused into the petals from bright red cup. A real show stopper. Height 14"–16". Late midseason bloomer.

'**Audubon**' Glistening white flower with rounded, overlapping, pressed petals. Coral-pink banded cup. Height 16"–18". Late midseason bloomer.

'**Avalon**' Rich lemon perianth, cup matures white. Strong, heavy substance resembling 'Camelot.' Good show flower. Height 16"–18". Late midseason bloomer.

'**Bantam**' Yellow flower with red/orange rim on cup. Intermediate sized. Ribbon winner, a real gem. Height 8"–10". Late midseason bloomer.

'**Berlin**' All yellow with large, frilled, red/orange-rimmed cup. Extremely showy. Height 15"–17". Late midseason bloomer.

'**Big Gun**' White petals and yellow-orange cup. Unusual and showy. American bred. Height 18"–20". Midseason bloomer.

'**Billy Graham**' Warm, soft yellow, overlapping petals with halo at base. Warm, pale coral-pink cup with scalloped edges. Show quality. Height 12"–16". Midseason bloomer.

'Bulley' Creamy yellow, rounded petals. Extremely frilled orange cup. Unusual, showy flower that packs a "punch" in the garden. Height 14"–16". Midseason bloomer.

'By George' Soft yellow, overlapping rounded petals. Peachy pink cup with darker pink edge frosted with a bit of white. One of the showiest flowers in our garden. Height 14"–16". Midseason bloomer.

'Camelot' Clear golden yellow show flower. One of the sturdiest, best, and latest-blooming yellows. Extremely heavy substance. Long-lasting. Height 14"–16". Late bloomer.

'Carlton' Two-toned yellow. Vanilla fragrance. The world's most numerous daffodil. Super perennializer everywhere, especially in the southern U. S. Forces well. Heirloom, 1927. Height 18"–20". Early midseason bloomer.

'Caruso' Deep yellow perianth. Broad orange-red, rimmed, sunproof cup. Large flower. Height 16"–18". Midseason bloomer.

'Ceylon' Strong yellow with orange-red cup. Extremely strong grower and perennializer. Sunproof. Our longest-lasting flower and one of our favorites. Height 14"–16". Early midseason bloomer.

'Chromacolor' Pure white petals. Large, deep coral-pink cup whose color intensifies with depth of cup. A real knockout. Height 14"–17". Mid-late season bloomer.

'Cool Flame' A genuine color-break cultivar having immaculate white petals and deep coral-pink cup. Good for show, garden, and picking. Height 18"–20". Late midseason bloomer.

'Curly' Two-toned yellow with unusual, extremely frilled cup. A show stopper. Height 16"–18". Midseason bloomer.

'Decoy' Listed as white petals, red cup, but in our garden cup is rich, deep coral pink. American-bred. Height 13"–16". Late midseason.

'Eastern Dawn' White petals, swept back, with apricot-pink cup. Exceptionally strong grower. A show flower. Height 14"–16". Late midseason bloomer.

'Fragrant Rose' Pure white petals. Reddish-pink cup with greenish-white eye. Perfectly formed flowers. Fragrant. Height 16"–18". Late bloomer.

'Delibes' Perianth resembles lemon hearts. A grand crimson-banded, flat-cupped flower looks as if it's been kissed. Good perennializer. Height 16"–18". Early midseason bloomer.

'Flower Record' White with yellow-and-red cup. One of the free-flowering reliables for perennializing. 1943. Height 16"–18". Midseason bloomer.

'Gigantic Star' Saffron yellow. Vanilla fragrance. Good perennializer. Excellent for zones 3–9. One of the best giant yellows in the South. Height 18"–20". Early midseason bloomer.

'Easter Moon' Stark white show flower. Height 18"–20". Midseason bloomer.

'Fortissimo' Yellow and red/orange flower. Gargantuan and showy. One of our largest offerings. Excellent with *Fritillaria imperialis* 'Rubra.' Height 18"–20". Late midseason bloomer.

'Glen Clova' Rich golden yellow perianth segments. Rich reddish-orange trumpetlike cup. Long-lasting showwinner. Height 16"–18". Midseason bloomer.

'High Fire' Golden, upfacing flower with overlapping petals. Solid orange-red cup. Blue ribbon flower, glows in the garden. Height 14"–16". Midseason bloomer.

'High Society' Ivory, hooded petals hug the white cup. Cup has green eye and pink rim. Lovely. Height 16"–18". Late bloomer.

'Ice Follies' Creamy white, extra-large flower with light yellow flat cup. One of the best perennializers. World's second most numerous daffodil. Forces well. Excellent with single early tulips and hyacinths. Height 16"–18". Early midseason bloomer.

'Impresario' Soft lemon yellow with a yellow-edged, white cup and halo. Elegant, blue ribbon flower. Height 14"–16". Midseason bloomer

'Johann Strauss' White petals with brilliant orange cup. Superb when forced. Needs shade outside to keep from burning. Height 16"–18". Early bloomer.

'Kissproof' Coppery, apricot-yellow petals with brick red flat cup. Floriferous, strong grower. Height 16"–18". Late midseason bloomer.

'Louise de Coligny' White and pink. Musky fragrance. Good perennializer. Height 14"–16". Midseason bloomer.

'Manon Lescaut' White petals with yellow and orange cup. Large and spectacular. Strong grower and show flower. Height 18"–20". Late midseason bloomer.

'Misty Glen' Opens pure white with satiny smooth perianths. Goblet-shaped cup. Strong, free-flowering. Height 16"–18". Late midseason bloomer.

'Modern Art' Strong yellow petals with a triple-frilled orange cup. A showy knockout. Height 16"–18". Midseason bloomer.

'Monal' Bright yellow petals. Vivid red-orange cup. Forces with little cold period. Height 16"–18". Early bloomer.

'Mon Cherie' White petals with frilled pink cup. A real beauty. Height 16"–18". Midseason bloomer.

'Passionale' White petals and extremely soft pink cup. Pressed petals. Show flower and good landscape perennial. Prolific. Height 16"–18". Late midseason bloomer.

'Peaches and Cream' Creamy petals with soft pastel peach cup. Large, extremely strong. Height 16"–18". Late midseason bloomer.

'Pimpernel' Rich golden perianth. Very large, deep tangerine, bowl-shaped cup with moderate frill on edge. Big, bold and showy. Excellent perennial. Height 18"–20". Midseason bloomer.

'Pink Charm' White petals with brilliant, large, dark orange-pink banded cup. Often 2 large flowers per stem. A show stopper, one of the best. Height 16"–18". Late midseason bloomer.

'Pink Pride' White petals, pink cup. Excellent garden plant. Height 18"–20". Midseason bloomer.

'Pinza' Rich golden yellow spade-shaped petals. Bright orange-red cup with golden-yellow center. Long-term landscape daffodil. Height 16"–18". Early midseason bloomer.

'Precocious' Pristine white petals. Very curly, flat, large cup in shades of bright coral-pink. Height 14"–17". Late midseason.

'Redhill' Ivory white with red-orange cup. Extremely strong, sunproof. A showy perennial. Has won "Best in Show" award! Height 16"–18". Late midseason bloomer.

'Romance' Pink cultivar, one of the finest show pinks. Excellent color, form, and substance. Vigorous grower. Height 16"–18". Late midseason bloomer.

'Roseworthy' White, slightly reflexed perianth. Midsized, frilled, rosy pink cup. Floriferous. Heirloom, 1950. Height 12"–14". Late bloomer.

'Rosy Wonder' White petals, broad band of pink in a slightly frilled cup. Exceptional variety, often 2 flowers per stem. Height 16"–18". Late midseason bloomer.

'Salome' Ivory white, light yellow trumpetlike cup that turns salmon pink. Good perennial and a blue-ribbon show winner. Height 16"–18". Late midseason bloomer.

'Scarlet O'Hara' A fine yellow and red/orange cup. Prolific. Excellent landscape perennial. Height 16"–18". Early midseason bloomer.

'Sentinel' Pink cultivar. Resembles a pink pinwheel or a pink-cupped giant 'Ice Follies.' One of the showiest garden flowers. American bred. Height 16"–18". Midseason bloomer.

'Serola' Bright deep yellow with dark orange-red cup. One of the latest varieties. Height 16"–18". Midseason bloomer.

'**Stainless**' Pristine white. Prolific, excellent grower. Show flower. Height 18"–20". Late bloomer.

'**St. Keverne**' All-yellow, superb grower, even in zones 8 and 9. Early forcer. Show flower. One of the best. Heirloom, 1934. Height 16"–18". Early bloomer.

'**St. Patrick's Day**' Primrose yellow with large flat cup that matures to white. An 'Ice Follies' seedling that almost glows. Height 16"–18". Midseason bloomer.

'**Virginia Sunrise**' Clear white perianth. Very bright, frilled, large, sunrise-orange cup. A winner in your landscape display. Height 18"–20". Midseason bloomer.

'**White Plume**' White perianth with white cup. One of the best landscape whites. Strong, up-facing, perennial grower. Show flower. Wonderful with blue Muscari or blue Hyacinthoides. Height 18"–20". Late bloomer.

DIVISION III: SMALL-CUPPED DAFFODILS

Overall characteristics: There is one flower to a stem. The cup or corona is not more than one-third the length of the perianth segments. These are long-term perennials good for naturalizing or as bedding plants. Excellent cultivars in Division III:

'**Barrett Browning**' White with orange-red cup, the earliest-blooming cultivar of this color. Strong substance. Forces well. Excellent for perennializing. Height 14"–16". Early bloomer.

'**Birma**' Dark yellow with vivid red/orange cup. Excellent for perennializing. Show flower. Needs partial shade. Height 16"–18". Early bloomer.

'Cherry Spot' Clear white, overlapping petals. Brilliant orange, flat cup that folds back against the petals. American-bred. Height 14"–17". Late midseason bloomer.

'Doctor Hugh' Creamy, overlapping petals. Small yellow and orange cup up to 4" across. Giant, poeticus-type flower. Fragrant. Long-lasting. Height 16"–18". Late season bloomer.

'Dreamlight' White petals. White cup with a red rim. Unmistakable show form. Height 16"–18". Late bloomer.

'Mint Julep' Palest yellow, rounded, overlapping perianth segments. Green-eyed cup. Outstanding for show and in the garden. Height 16"–18". Late midseason bloomer.

'Polar Ice' All-white flower suitable for heirloom gardens. Heirloom, 1936. Height 14"–16". Late midseason bloomer.

'Sabine Hay' Brilliant copper-orange perianth with dramatic red cup. A show stopper. Height 16"–18". Late midseason bloomer.

'Sinopel' All-white perianth with unusual yellow-rimmed green cup. Fragrant. Height 16"–18". Extremely late bloomer.

DIVISION IV. DOUBLE DAFFODILS

Overall characteristics: These are the double and the roselike flowers. Both single and multiple blooms have been show winners. These are vivid plants good for bedding and picking, provided they receive protection from the wind. Excellent cultivars in Division IV:

'Abba' White with orange segments. Double sport of 'Cragford.' Multiflowered. Forces with minimal cold period. Exceptionally musky fragrance. Height 16"–18". Early midseason bloomer.

'Acropolis' Pure white with creases of crimson. Very full, beautiful single show flower with great substance. Height 18"–20". Late-midseason bloomer.

'Delnashaugh' White, very large, overlapping, rounded petals that surround a tight cluster of apricot-pink inner segments. Hybrid of 'Romance'. Height 16"–18". Late bloomer.

'Flower Drift' Ivory white with yellow-orange segments. Single flowered. Superb perennializer. A sport of 'Flower Record.' Height 14"–16". Late midseason bloomer.

'Bridal Crown' Cream and saffron, multiple blooms. Earliest-blooming double. Strongly fragrant. One of the best for forcing or container growing. Height 14"–16". Early midseason bloomer.

'Erlicheer' White and yellow show flower. 15-20 florets per stem. Extremely fragrant. Great forcer, excellent in pots. Good for zones 6 through 9. Height 12"–14". Early midseason bloomer.

'Ice King' White petals with double yellow cup. Single flowered, showy, double 'Ice Follies' sport that sometimes reverts to original characteristics. Height 16"–18". Early midseason bloomer.

'Cheerfulness' White with light-yellow flecks. Multiflowered, fragrant. Excellent perennializer. Heirloom, 1923. Height 14"–16". Late bloomer.

'Exotic Beauty' Creamy white, overlapping perianth segments. Long, narrow, trumpet-like cup. Slightly flared at end, filled with rose-pink petaloids. Height 13"–17". Late-midseason bloomer.

'Innovator' Warm bronzy-yellow, double petals interspersed throughout with orange, frilled sepals. Strong stems. Height 14"–17". Midseason bloomer.

'Madison' Color of a "Dreamsicle" popsicle with whipped cream. Double form of *N.* 'Sweet Charity'. Fragrant. Height 14"–16". Midseason bloomer.

'Manly' Creamy yellow with mandarin orange petals. Single-flowered. Unusual, pretty, and strong. Good perennial. Height 12"–14". Late midseason bloomer.

'Obdam' Almost pure-white, fully double sport of 'Ice Follies'. Excellent in the evening garden. Height 16"–18". Midseason bloomer.

'Pink Paradise' Pure white and rose-pink, single-flowered. Durable in the garden. Height 16"–18". Midseason bloomer.

'Sir Winston Churchill' Creamy white with orange petals. Multiflowered. Robust, fragrant sport of 'Geranium' cultivar. Perennializer, one of the best. Height 15"–16". Late bloomer.

'Tahiti' Sulfur yellow with red petals. Strong stem. Superior display plant with one extremely large flower per stem. Show flower. Perennializer. Height 12"–14". Late midseason bloomer.

'Telamonius Plenus' (Syn. Van Sion). Pale yellow perianth segments. Cup often filled with extra petaloids the first season. Rumpled appearance thereafter. Variable. Heirloom, 1620; zones 3-9. Height 12"–14". Early bloomer.

'White Lion' Thick, creamy white outer petaloids interspersed with shorter, soft yellow segments. Durable, long-term perennial. Heirloom, 1949. Height 18"–20". Midseason bloomer.

'Yellow Cheerfulness' Yellow, fragrant, multiflowered. Excellent perennializer. Heirloom, 1937. Height 14"–16". Late bloomer.

DIVISION V:
TRIANDRUS DAFFODILS

Overall characteristics: There are 2–3 nodding, pendulous blossoms per stem, like fuchsias. All have a fruity fragrance. These graceful perennializers are good for picking as well as for container plantings, borders, and rock gardens. Excellent cultivars in Division V:

'Ice Wings' Pure ivory white show flower also excellent in pots. 2–3 long-lasting flowers per stem. Height 12"–14". Early midseason bloomer.

'Lemon Drops' Two-toned yellow, large, teardrop-shaped flowers, 2–3 per stem. American-bred. Height 12"–14". Midseason bloomer.

'Petrel' Pure white, heavily fragrant. The most floriferous with 3–5 florets. Show flower. American bred. Height 14"–16". Late midseason bloomer.

'Stint' Soft, luminous yellow. 2–3 flowers per stem. Excellent garden plant and show flower. American bred. Height 12"–14". Midseason bloomer.

'Thalia' Whitest of whites. Fragrant, superb garden perennial with 2–3 blossoms. Heirloom, 1916. Height 12"–14". Late midseason bloomer.

DIVISION VI:
CYCLAMINEUS DAFFODILS

Overall characteristics: These have a graceful, trumpetlike cup with flared-back petals and small leaves. Good for forcing and for perennializing, these cultivars perform well in rock gardens and borders, in planters and window boxes. They are extremely early bloomers. Excellent cultivars in Division VI:

'The Alliance' All-yellow show flower with outstanding substance. Strong, American bred. Height 12"–14". Early bloomer.

'Beryl' Straw-colored, orange-banded, elfin show flower with a short cup. Heirloom, 1907. Height 7"–9". Midseason bloomer.

'Carib' White, recurved petals. Long, medium-pink cup flares at the end. A prizewinner. Height 12"–14". Midseason bloomer.

'February Gold' Sulfur yellow with yellow-orange cup. Excellent for forcing and perennializing. Good choice for patio planters and window boxes. Heirloom, 1923. Height 12"–14". Extremely early bloomer.

'Foundling' White flower with swept-back petals and rose-pink cup. Graceful, small. A sturdy plant and good increaser. Exceptional show flower. Height 10"–12". Late midseason bloomer.

'Itzim' Yellow and red cultivar, dramatically reflexed petals. Develops color after opening. Long-lasting, show flower. American bred. Height 12"–14". Early bloomer.

'Jack Snipe' White cultivar having crisp, overlapping rounded white petals with gently fringed yellow cup. Intermediate size. A pert little show flower. Height 8"–10". Midseason bloomer.

'Jenny' Opens creamy, matures to strong all-white garden plant that also wins ribbons in shows. Height 10"–12". Midseason bloomer.

'Jetfire' Red-orange with yellow cup. Spectacular, often produces secondary blooms. One of the best. American bred. Height 12"–14". Midseason bloomer.

'Kaydee' White petals. Vivid salmon-pink cup. Pinkest of the pink cyclamineus. Height 10"–12". Midseason bloomer.

'Larkwhistle' Golden blossoms resembling its namesake in flight. Flower stands well above the leaves. Show flower. Height 12"–14". Midseason bloomer.

'Lemon Silk' Opens with pale yellow petals and medium-yellow cup that matures to pure white. Height 10"–12". Early midseason bloomer.

'Lilac Charm' White, glistening, reflexed petals may show greenish blush at base. Lilac/pink, trumpet-like cup. Very unusual. Height 12"–14". Midseason bloomer.

'Little Princess' White perianth. Rich deep-salmon cup. Ideal for pot or window box. Height 10"–12". Mid-late season bloomer.

'Phalarope' Creamy-white, pointy, overlapping, very recurved petals. Stovepipe, yellow cup. Very elegant. Height 10"–12". Late midseason bloomer.

'Surfside' Ivory perianth with white cup. Large show flower. American bred. Height 12"–14". Midseason bloomer.

'Tracey' All white, graceful show flower. New Zealand-bred beauty. Height 12"–14". Midseason bloomer.

'Wheater' Yellow, pointed petals with a white halo at the base. Long, narrow, pure white cup. One of the few reverse-bicolors in this division. Height 12"–14". Midseason bloomer.

DIVISION VII: JONQUILLA DAFFODILS

Overall characteristics: There are several small flowers per stem, with a fragrance resembling honeysuckle or jasmine. The leaves are dark green, almost reedlike, and are smaller than most daffodil leaves. These cultivars are good perennializers that prefer hot summers. They are adapted to the Deep South (zones 8 and 9), but also do well in zones 5–7. They make a good picked flower and are recommended for use in beds and rock gardens. Excellent cultivars of Division VII:

'Bell Song' Ivory white and pink. 3–5 flowers per stem. Fragrant. American bred. Height 12"–14". Late bloomer.

'Bunting' Yellow petals with bright orange cup. 2–4 flowers per stem. American bred show flower. Height 12"–14". Late bloomer.

'Divertimento' White petals. Coral-pink cup. Narrow, dark-green foliage. American-bred. Floriferous. Fragrant. Height 14"–16". Late midseason bloomer.

'Fruit Cup' White and pale yellow. Large cup. Perfect form. American-bred hybrid. Fragrant. Height 10"–12". Late midseason bloomer.

'Hillstar' Canary yellow petals, white halo with ivory white cups. 2–3 showy flowers per stem. Show flower that sets seed. American bred. Height 14"–16". Late midseason bloomer.

'Intrigue' Bright yellow perianth segments with halo. Pure white, broad cup, scalloped on the edge. A bit variable. Height 14"–16". Late bloomer.

'Kedron' Several vivid orange cups "bleed" their color into the rich bronzy-yellow, perfectly formed petals. Fragrant. Height 12"–15". Midseason bloomer.

'Key Lime' Registered as all white, but has a greenish hue that reminds us of key lime pie. Our own hybrid. Tons of flowers. Blooms well above foliage. Fragrant. Height 12"–14". Mid-late season bloomer.

'Pappy George' Bright amber-yellow petals. Deep reddish-orange cups. Two to three flowers per stem. Floriferous. Fragrant. One of our own, named for Brent's father. Height 14"–16". Midseason bloomer.

'Pink Angel' Sparkling white petals. Soft-pink edged white cup with green eye. Dainty-looking, but strong, prolific. Height 14"–16". Late bloomer.

'Pipit' Pale yellow, 2–3 flowers per stem, each with a white cup. Unusual and long-lasting. American bred, show-winning perennial. Height 14"–16". Midseason bloomer.

'Pueblo' All white, lots of flowers. Fragrant. American-bred. Height 12"–14". Late bloomer.

'Punchline' Palest yellow petals. Small, broad cup of same color matures with pink rim. Lots of flowers. Fragrant. Height 14"–16". Midseason bloomer.

'Quail' Rich bronzy yellow, multiflowered. Long-lasting improved cultivar of 'Sweetness.' American bred. One of the best. Height 12"–14". Midseason bloomer.

'Sailboat' Creamy white flowers with swept-back petals. Long-cupped. Numerous flowers. Fragrant. Height 10"–12". Late midseason bloomer.

'Stratosphere' All yellow, 2–4 flowers per stem. Tall, floriferous, and dramatic. Beautiful form with outstanding fragrance. Show flower. American bred. Height 18"–20". Late midseason bloomer.

'Suzy' Yellow petals with flat, brick red cups. Several perky blossoms per stem. Sunproof color. Height 15"–17". Midseason bloomer.

'Sweetness' Yellow cultivar having 1–2 yellow blossoms per stem. Superb perennializer and prolific grower. Produces secondary flowers and excels in fragrance. Forces well. Heirloom, 1939. Height 12"–14". Midseason bloomer.

'Trevithian' Deep yellow, slightly curled petals with a faintly frilled flat cup. 2–3 flowers per stem. Fragrant. Superb landscape plant. Heirloom, 1927. Height 16"–18". Early midseason bloomer.

DIVISION VIII:
TAZETTA DAFFODILS

Overall characteristics: There are many pungent flowers per stem. The fragrance of these is musky sweet. They are excellent perennializers that perform well in southern areas, zones 5–9. In northern regions, including Canada, provide more protection. Recommended for forcing, bedding, and picking. Excellent cultivars of Division VIII:

'Avalanche' Glistening white petals and yellow cups, 15–20 flowers per stem. A cultivar of 'Seventeen Sisters.' Show flower. Use also in restoration gardens in zones 6 through 9. Heirloom, 1700. Height 16"–18". Midseason bloomer.

'Canarybird' Yellow petals with dull orange cups. 3–5 flowers per stem. Height 14"–16". Late midseason bloomer.

'Cragford' Bright white petals with charming orange cups. 3–5 rounded flowers per stem. Forces easily without cold period. Fragrant and hardy in zone 5. Heirloom, 1930. Height 12"–14". Early midseason bloomer.

'Falconet' Yellow petals with brick red cups. 3–5 flowers per stem. Strong fragrance. Show flower. American bred. Height 12"–14". Late midseason bloomer.

'Geranium' White and orange, 3–5 flowers per stem. Good perennializer. Long-lasting, late forcer. Heirloom, 1930. Height 15"–17". Late midseason bloomer.

'Golden Dawn' Golden cultivar having orange cups. 3–5 flowers per stem. Perennializer. Dark green leaves on this show flower. Hardy in zones 5 through 9. Height 14"–16". Midseason bloomer.

'Highfield Beauty' Soft yellow blossoms with orange-banded rims. 2–3 flowers per stem. A show flower, Australian bred. The largest tazetta. Height 18"–20". Late midseason bloomer.

'Hoopoe' Yellow petals with orange cups. 3–5 blossoms per stem. Good multiplier with strong fragrance. American bred. Height 15"–17". Late midseason bloomer.

'Laurens Koster' Sports 3-5 creamy white florets with flat yellowish-orange cups. Height 12"–14". Heirloom, 1909. Fragrant. Midseason bloomer.

'Martinette' Bright yellow and orange. Many small flowers. Very fragrant. Height 14"–16". Early-midseason bloomer.

'Scarlet Gem' Bright saffron petals slightly folded together around flat, frilled-edge, red-orange cups. 3–5 flowers per stem. Show flower. Heirloom, 1910. Height 14"–16". Late midseason bloomer.

NONHARDY TAZETTAS

These cultivars can be forced without a cold period and many can be successfully grown outdoors in zones 8 and 9. Like other tazettas they have many pungent flowers per stem and a musky, sweet fragrance.

'Bethlehem' (Syn. Nony). Soft yellow petals with a barium yellow cup. Delicate, musky fragrance. One of the paper-whites. Height 8"–10". 3 weeks to bloom.

'Chinese Sacred Lily' White petals with yellow cups. Pleasant fragrance. Requires stem support. Not technically a paper-white, but similar in character. Height 10"–14". 3–4 weeks to bloom.

'Constantinople' Double form of 'Chinese Sacred Lily' with same coloring, fragrance and growth habit. Height 12"–20". 3-4 weeks to bloom.

'Galilee' (Syn. Gallilea). Pure white. Moderate musky fragrance. Height 12"–14". 3 weeks to bloom.

'Grand Soleil d'Or' Lemon to gold florets, yellow to orange cup. Delicate, sweet fragrance. Height 12"–14". 4–5 weeks to bloom.

'Israel' (Syn. Omri). Creamy yellow petals, sulfur yellow cup. Delicate musky fragrance. Strong stems. One of the paper-whites. Height 16"–20". 3 weeks to bloom.

'Jerusalem' (Syn. Sheleg). Pure white. The largest florets, strongest stems. Moderate musky fragrance. One of the paper-whites. Height 16"–20". 3 weeks to bloom.

'Nazareth' (Syn. Yael). Soft yellow petals, bright yellow cup. Moderate musky fragrance. One of the paper-whites. Height 10"–12". 3 weeks to bloom.

'Ziva' Pure white. Very rapid growth, easy to force. Strong musky fragrance. One of the paper-whites. Height 14"–18". 2 weeks to bloom.

DIVISION IX: POETICUS DAFFODILS

Overall characteristics: These have dogwoodlike, white blossoms with red-rimmed, yellow cups. Their fragrance is spicy. This cultivar is recommended for picking, perennializing, or for border plantings, especially in the cooler climates. Excellent cultivars of Division IX:

'Actaea' White, prim, rounded petals with dark red, banded, yellow cup. Excellent perennial. Show flower named for one of King Solomon's concubines. Heirloom, 1927. Height 15"–17". Late midseason bloomer.

'Dactyl' Rounded, flat, white flower. Small cup of deep gold with a green eye and dark-red ribbon of a rim. Height 12"–14". Late bloomer.

'Felindre' White petals with a green, yellow, and red cup. Striking show flower. Heirloom, 1930. Height 16"–18". Late bloomer.

'Milan' White petals with green, yellow, and red cup. Graceful show flower. Heirloom, 1932. Height 16"–18". Late bloomer.

DIVISION X: BULBOCODIUM

The characteristics of this group are clearly evident: Usually one flower to a stem. Perianth segments are insignificant compared with the dominant corona or cup, which often looks like a megaphone. Anthers are attached more or less centrally to the filament. Filament and style are usually curved.

'Golden Bells' Rich golden-yellow, funnel-shaped cup with narrow, star-like petals. Four to eight perfect "hoop petticoats" from each bulb. Excellent for pots and forcing. Height 4"–6". Midseason bloomer.

'Kenellis' White petals. "Megaphone" yellow cup. Unusual form. Intermediate-size flower. Height 5"–6". Late midseason bloomer.

DIVISION XI: SPLIT-CORONA DAFFODILS

DIVISION XI-A: COLLAR TYPES

Overall characteristics: The corona, or cup, is split for at least one-third of its length. Large, upfacing blossoms make this one of the showiest groups for mass plantings in the landscape. They are also excellent flowers for picking and arranging. Excellent cultivars of Division XI:

'Belcanto' Creamy white; matures to soft lemon with a hint of pink in the frilled corona. Height 18"–20". Late midseason bloomer.

'Blanc de Blancs' Opens with yellow in the cup, matures to pure white. Shape almost flat against perianth segments. Sturdy stems. Height 15"–17". Midseason bloomer.

'Cassata' White petals with ruffled lemon cup maturing to milky white. Forces and perennializes well. Height 16"–18". Early midseason bloomer.

'Colblanc' Pure white collar with green eye. Unusual. Height 14"–16". Midseason bloomer.

'Cum Laude' White petals with yellow and salmon pink, very frilled collar. A show stopper. Height 14"–16". Midseason bloomer.

'Flyer' Rich bright-yellow cup almost covers its petals. Probably the most frilled and ruffled split-corona daffodil available. Height 12"–14". Late midseason bloomer.

'Mary Gay Lirette' Opens with yellow cup, quickly turning salmon, folding back against white petals. Sturdy. Floriferous. Height 14"–16". Early midseason bloomer.

'Mondragon' Golden yellow petals with deep orange collar. An applelike fragrance. Height 14"–16". Midseason bloomer.

'Orangery' Creamy white with orange collar. Height 14"–16". Early midseason bloomer.

'Palmares' Smooth white perianth, solid pink-frilled collar. Height 14"–16". Late midseason bloomer.

'Paradise Island' Dominant three sepals on cream and salmon flower appear as triangles in the garden. Strong grower. Height 15"–19". Midseason bloomer.

'Printal' Frilled yellow cultivar, striking. Earliest split type to bloom in our field. Excellent for forcing. Height 16"–18". Early midseason bloomer.

'Rosado' Creamy white, spreading perianth segments. Coral-pink cup folds back against perianth. Lots of flowers. Height 14"–16". Midseason bloomer.

'Smiling Face' Clear white perianth almost covered by rich yellow-ruffled corona. Attention-getter. Height 13"–17". Midseason bloomer.

'Sovereign' White petals with orange collar. Very large. Height 16"–18". Late midseason bloomer.

'Tricollet' White petals with orange corona. A breakthrough in form with its corona divided into thirds. Height 14"–16". Late midseason bloomer.

'Tripartite' Lemon-yellow flowers. Short, flat, split coronas. Like a cluster of butterflies. Sports 3-4 flowers to a stem. Fragrant. Height 12"–14". Mid-late season.

DIVISION XI-B:
PAPILLON TYPES

Cultivars of these split-corona daffodils are known as "butterfly" types. They have a sunburst of color out from the center of the cup.

'Broadway Star' White petals with orange-rayed white corona. Height 14"–16". Late midseason bloomer.

'Burning Heart' Yellow petals, orange collar with white edge. Height 14"–16". Late-midseason bloomer.

'Firestreak' Creamy white petals, creamy cup with red flames. Height 14"–16". Midseason bloomer.

'Lemon Beauty' Starch-white petals. Creamy white cup with bright rays of sunlight-yellow in its center. It glows. Height 15"–17". Midseason bloomer.

'Papillon Blanc' White with sunbursts of green and yellow. Height 17"–18". Late bloomer.

'Sorbet' Ivory white with sunbursts of yellow-orange. Height 15"–16". Late midseason bloomer.

'Space Shuttle' White petals, yellow corona. A show winner. Height 16"–18". Late midseason bloomer.

DIVISION XII OTHER

This group includes all daffodil cultivars that do not fit the definition of any other division. Excellent cultivars of Division XII:

'Bittern' Lovely, bold yellow reflexed petals. Several small, rich-orange cups. Not at all shy or retiring like its namesake bird. Graceful, showy, mid-sized flower. Height 10"–12". Late midseason.

DIVISION XIII: SPECIES AND WILD FORMS

Overall characteristics: This group includes all species, wild forms, and wild hybrids suitable for use in berms, rock gardens, in naturalized settings, and among short ground-covers. These species are also suitable for restoration (18th-century) gardens. Excellent cultivars of Division XIII:

N. ×medioluteus (Syn. *×biflorus*) White petals with yellow cups. 1–2 fragrant flowers. A wild hybrid of *N. poeticus* var. *recurvus* and *N. tazetta.* Also called "Twin Sisters." Height 12"–14". Very late bloomer.

N. bulbocodium var. ***conspicuus*** All yellow megaphone-shaped cup with reedlike petals. Will often reseed in acid soil. Excellent for shows, forcing, in pots, and in the lawn. Also called "Hoop Petticoat." Height 4"–6". Midseason bloomer.

N. jonquilla Gold petals and gold cup. The most fragrant flower in this division. Grows best in acid soil that gets a summer baking. Excellent in scree, near rocks, walls, or walkways. 3–5 flowers per stem. Grasslike, dark green foliage. Naturalized throughout the Southeast. Also a show flower. Often called "Simplex." Height 6"–8". Midseason bloomer.

N. ×odorus Linnaeus (Syn. *campernellii.*) Medium yellow petals and cup. 2–3 flowers per stem. *Jonquilla* type. A cross between *N. jonquilla* and *N. pseudonarcissus.* Very fragrant. Height 10"–12". Early bloomer.

N. ×odorus flore pleno (syn. var. *plenus*). Yellow. 2–3 fragrant flowers per stem. Sport of *odorus*. Also called "Queen Anne's Double Jonquil." Height 10"–12". Early bloomer.

N. pseudonarcissus **subsp.** *obvallaris* Golden yellow trumpet. Forces well, excellent in pots. From Great Britain. Also called "Tenby." Height 8"–10". Very early bloomer.

N. pseudonarcissus **subsp.** *moschatus* All white trumpet. Lovely, nodding variety. Also called "Silver Bells" or "Swans Neck Daffodil." Height 8"–10". Early midseason bloomer.

N. poeticus **var.** *recurvus* White poeticus petals with red-rimmed, yellow cup. Spicy fragrance. Excellent particularly in zones 3–7. Also called "Pheasant's-Eye." Height 10"–13". Very late bloomer.

MINIATURES

Various divisions: These tiny cultivars and varieties may be found in many divisions and are often 6" tall or shorter. They are excellent for use at the front of a garden border or in the niches of tree roots. They perform well in rock gardens, window boxes, and patio containers and are reliable for perennializing and forcing. Excellent cultivars of miniatures:

'Baby Moon' Div. 7. Yellow flowers. Multiflowered, very fragrant. This is a selected form of *N. jonquilla*. Height 10"–12". Late midseason bloomer.

'Canaliculatus' Div. 8. White petals with golden cups. 5–7 sweetly fragrant florets per stem. Requires summer heat. Forces like a paper-white. Show flower. Height 4"–6". Early midseason bloomer.

'Chit Chat' Div. 7. All yellow, *jonquilla* type. Prolific, American bred. Height 3"–4". Late midseason bloomer.

'Fairy Chimes' Div. 5. Dainty, goblet-shaped, chartreuse-yellow flowers. Usually 6–8 per stem. Strong grower. Height 4"–6". Late midseason bloomer.

'**Golden Quince**' Div. 12. Golden version and sport of *N.* 'Quince' with similar characteristics and growing habits. Zones 4–8. Height 5"–6". Midseason bloomer.

'**Hawera**' Div. 5. Pale yellow elfin bells, several flowers per stem, each with swept-back petals. Triandrus type. Outstanding forcer and perennializer from New Zealand. Heirloom, 1938. Height 8"–10". Late bloomer.

'**Jumblie**' Div. 12. Canary yellow petals with yellow-orange cup. Reflexed petals. A multiflowering cyclamineus sibling of 'Tete-a-Tete.' Height 5"–6". Late midseason bloomer.

'**Little Beauty**' Div. 1. White and sulfur yellow trumpet. An easy forcer. Height 5"–6". Early bloomer.

'**Little Gem**' Div. 1. Yellow petals with yellow trumpet. An easy forcer. Heirloom, 1938. Height 4"–5". Early bloomer.

'**Little Rusky**' Div. 7. Pale yellow, overlapping, rounded petals. Green-eyed, yellow cup with light orange rim. Fragrant. Show flower. Zones 5–9. Height 4"–6". Midseason bloomer.

'**Midget**' Div. 10. All yellow trumpet. A selection of *N. nanus*. Height 4"–5". Early midseason bloomer.

'**Minnow**' Div. 8. Variable, multi-hued white petals surround bright buttercup centers. Multiflowering tazetta type. Height 5"–6". Midseason bloomer.

'**Mite**' Div. 6. All yellow cyclameneus type. Vigorous, a little larger than most miniatures. Height 5"–6". Early midseason bloomer.

nanus* var. *lobularis Div. 13. Soft yellow, narrow petals. Long, flared, rich golden-yellow trumpet. This has naturalized and made a wonderful addition to our meadow. Height 6"–8". Early bloomer.

'Pencrebar' Div. 4. Saffron yellow. Petite, fragrant double flowers. Heirloom, 1929. Height 5"–6". Midseason bloomer.

'Rikki' Div. 7. Creamy white petals, yellow cup. Very variable. Height 4"–6". Late midseason bloomer.

'New-Baby' Div. 7. A bicolored *N.* 'Baby Moon' with similar, easy growing habits. Sweet fragrance. Height 4"–8". Very late season bloomer.

'Picoblanco' Div. 2. Large cup, proud, upfacing flower of clear white with a creamy white cup. Great for rock garden, protected garden niche. Height 4"–6". Late midseason bloomer.

'Rip van Winkle' (Syn. *N. pumilus* var. *plenus*). Div. 4. Double, variable, old-fashioned yellow flower resembling a dandelion. All yellow with green segments interspersed. Heirloom, 1884. Height 4"–6". Early midseason bloomer.

'Pacific Coast' Div. 8. An all yellow form of *N.* 'Minnow.' Very prolific, many florets per stem. Zones 5–9. Height 5"–6". Midseason bloomer.

'Quince' Div. 12. Sulfur yellow, 2–3 cyclamineus florets per stem. A sister seedling of 'Tete-a-Tete' and 'Jumblie.' Height 5"–6". Midseason bloomer.

'Segovia' Div. 3. White and yellow small cup, beautifully formed. One of the best. Height 8"–10". Midseason bloomer.

'Sundial' Div. 7. Yellow with green eyes. 1-2 tiny flat-cupped, jonquilla-type blooms. Height 4"–5". Late bloomer.

'Sun Disc' Div. 7. Buttercup yellow jonquilla-type. Very rounded perianth. A *Garden Week* selection. Height 5"–7". Very late bloomer.

'Tete-a-Tete' Div. 12. Buttercup yellow petals with yellowish orange corona. Excellent forcer. Height 5"–6". Early bloomer.

willkommii Div. 13. Jonquilla with 1 or 2 rich golden-yellow, petite flowers. Very dark green, round leaves. One of the smallest. Distinguished solely by botanical name. Unique for rock garden. Height 3"–4". Mid-late season bloomer.

'W. P. Milner' Div. 1. Creamy trumpet with corkscrew petals and frilled cup. Old-fashioned variety, Heirloom, 1869. Height 6"–8". Early midseason bloomer.

Sources for Bulbs

Here is an alphabetized list of sources for gardens and growers specializing in daffodil cultivars:

Bonnie Brae Gardens. 1105 SE Christensen Rd., Corbelt OR 97019. Frank and Jeanie Driver. Good selection of novelty and intermediate daffodils. Catalog free.

Brent and Becky's Bulbs. 7463 Heath Trail, Gloucester VA 23061. Brent and Becky Heath. Most extensive collection in the United States of daffodils available for show, garden, mass planting, and naturalizing. More than 400 cultivars, wholesale and retail. Ten-acre display garden open by appointment for tours in the spring. Our daffodils are displayed in most major public gardens. Catalog free. Toll-free (877) 661-2852. www.brentandbeckysbulbs.com

Cascade Daffodils. P.O. Box 237, Silverton, OR 97381-0237. Dave and Linda Karnstedt. Broad selection of 300 to 400 cultivars for the collector. Catalog $2.00.

Charles Mueller Co. 7091 N. River Rd., New Hope PA 18938. Charles Fritz and Nancy Gregory. Older company offering a good selection of novelty daffodils and a lovely display garden. Catalog free.

Cherry Creek Daffodils. Steve Vinisky, 21700 S.W. Chapman Rd., Sherwood, OR 97140-8608.

Grant Mitsch Novelty Daffodils. P. O. Box 218, Hubbard OR 97032. Elise and Dick Havens. Some of the finest daffodils of the past 50 years have been developed on this farm. Illustrated catalog shows hybrids developed by this family across three generations. Catalog $3.00.

Mary Mattison von Schaik. P. O. Box 32, Cavendish VT 05142. Paula M. Parker. Good selection of novelty daffodils. Catalog $1.00.

McClure and Zimmerman. P.O. Box 368. Friesland WI 53935. Broad selection of daffodils and other bulbs. Catalog free.

Nancy Wilson Species and Miniature Narcissus. 6525 Briceland-Thorn Road, Garberville CA 95440. Nancy Wilson. Good selection of seed-grown and nursery-propagated species of *Narcissus*. Catalog $1.00.

Oakwood Daffodils. 2330 W. Bertrand Rd., Niles MI 49120. Dr. John Reed. A specialist's listing of daffodils. Many choice cultivars. Catalog free.

Oregon Trail Daffodils. 41905 SE Louden Rd, Corbett OR 97019 Bill and Diane Tribe. Specializing in hybrids developed by Murray Evans and Bill Pannill. Some extremely fine cultivars. Catalog free.

Other company catalogs listing daffodil bulbs include Dutch Gardens, Jacques Amand, John Scheepers, K. van Bourgondien, Old House Garden, Park Seed Company, Van Dykes Flower Farms, Van Engelen Inc., W. Atlee Burpee, Wayside Gardens, and White Flower Farm.

An old tobacco barn on the edge of a trial field serves as the office of Brent and Becky's Bulbs.

Daffodil Societies

The American Daffodil Society,
Naomi Liggett, 4126 Winfield Rd.,
Columbus, OH 43220

Local Daffodil Societies
Adena Daffodil Society,
Mary Rutledge, 704 Ashley Dr.,
Chillicothe, OH 45601

Arkansas Daffodil Society,
J.A. Strauss, 322 Hall Street,
Malvern, AR 72104

'Pink Charm,' 'Dickcissel,' and hyacinth offer contrast in this picture painted with bulbs.

Central Ohio Daffodil Society,
Naomi Liggett, 4126 Winfield, Rd.,
Columbus, OH 43220

Central Mississippi Daffodil Society,
Dr. Ted Snazelle, 4418 McDonald
Dr., Clinton, MS 29056

Central Washington Daffodil Group,
Sonja Razey, 1686 Cleman Dr.,
Naches, WA 98937

Daffodil and Hosta Society of Western Pennsylvania, Toby Exter,
5328 Overlook Glen Dr.,
Pittsburgh, PA 15236

Daffodil Society of Minnesota,
Michael Berrigan,
2149 Hallmark Ave. N.,
Oakdale, MN 55126-4523

Delaware Valley Daffodil Society,
Mrs. Marvin Andersen,
7 Perth Dr.,
Wilmington, DE 19803

East Tennessee Daffodil Society,
Mrs. Lynn Ladd,
1701 Westcliff Dr.,
Maryville, TN 37801-6301

Florida Daffodil Society,
Linda Van Beck,
6061 Weeping Willow Way,
Tallahassee, FL 32311

Georgia Daffodil Society,
Bonnie Campbell, 590 Sandy
Creek Rd., Fayetteville, GA 30214

Greater St. Louis Daffodil Society,
Jason Delaney, 4344 Shaw Blvd.,
St. Louis, MO 63110

Greenwich Daffodil Society,
Nancy Mott, 38 Perkins Rd.,
Greenwich, CT 06830

Heart of Dixie Daffodil Society,
Weldon Childers, P.O. Box 188,
Carbon Hill, AL 35549

Indiana Daffodil Society,
Joe Hamm, 4815 Fauna Lane,
Indianapolis, IN 46234

Kentucky Daffodil Society,
Mrs. Hilda Dunaway,
3104 McMahan Blvd., Louisville,
KY 40220

Maryland Daffodil Society,
Joan George, 614 W. Timonium
Rd., Timonium, MD 21093

Middle Tennessee Daffodil Society,
Mary Cartwright,
1016 St. Andrews Place,
Nashville, TN 37204-4100

Midwest Daffodil Society,
George Dorner, 20753 N. Buffalo
Run, Kildeer, IL 60047

New Jersey Daffodil Society,
Elizabeth Ellwood, 12 Auldwood
Lane, Rumson, NJ 07760

North Carolina Daffodil Society,
Betsy Hackney, 104 Carolina
Forest, Chapel Hill, NC 27516

Northeast Ohio Daffodil Society,
Doug Fuhrmeyer, 7101 Schoepf
Dr., Northfield, OH 44067

Northern California Daffodil Society,
Bob Spotts, 409 Hazelnut Dr.,
Oakley, CA 94561

Northern Illinois Daffodil Society,
Nancy Pilipuf, 11090 Woodstock
Rd., Garden Prairie, IL 61038

*Northern New England Daffodil
Society*, Julie S. Crocker,
P.O. Box 500, Dublin, NH 03444

Oregon Daffodil Society,
Betty Forster, 31875 Fayetteville
Rd., Shedd, OR 97377

Southwestern Ohio Daffodil Society,
Bill Lee, 4606 Honeyhill Lane,
Batavia, OH 45103-1315

Texas Daffodil Society,
Mrs. Donald Sable, 4301
Edmondson, Dallas, TX 75205

Tuscarora Daffodil Group,
Richard Ezell, 334 Baltimore St.,
Gettysburg, PA 17325

Virginia Daffodil Society,
George Bragdon, 8702 Shadow
Lane, Richmond, VA 23229

Washington Daffodil Society,
Kathy Welsh, 10803 Windcloud
Ct., Oakton, VA 22124

Western Reserve Daffodil Society,
Dan Bellinger, 341 Akron Rd.,
Wadsworth, OH 44281

Wichita Daffodil Society,
Margie Roehr, 594 N. Broadway,
Wichita, KS 67206

Important International Societies
The Daffodil Society,
John Pearson, Hofflands,
Little Totham Rd., Goldhanger,
Maldon, Essex CM9 8AP, U.K.

*The National Daffodil Society of New
Zealand,* Wilf Hall, Fencourt Road,
RD 1, Cambridge 2351, New
Zealand. "For Daffodil Enthusiasts
the world over."

The Royal Horticulture Society. 80
Vincent Square 1, London England
SWIP ZPE. This is the
organization in charge of
registering all new cultivars.

*'Milan' contrasts nicely with the tulip
'Negrita.'*

Recommended Reading

Any of the publications below can be ordered from Brent and Becky's Bulbs, 7463 Heath Trail, Gloucester VA 23061, or from the American Daffodil Society, 1686 Gray Fox Trails, Milford OH 45150.

The American Daffodil Society. *The Daffodil Journal*. Quarterly publication with many fine articles by amateur gardeners and exhibitors. A few color photographs and a great deal of information about shows and winners. Increasing number of articles written for home gardeners.

The American Daffodil Society. *The Daffodil Data Bank*, Yearly. A list of the parentage of all known daffodil hybrids as well as information on many cultivars no longer in cultivation. This is especially helpful to hybridizers.

The American Daffodil Society. *Daffodils to Show and Grow*, 1999. A checklist of more than 5,000 currently grown cultivars and species. Brief coded information includes name of the breeder, the Royal Horticultural Society classification, the blooming season, average height, fertility, and the year introduced. Helpful for persons interested in entering flowers to show.

A "rug" of 'Daydream' daffodils under magnolias at the Arnold Arboretum creates an atmosphere conducive to outdoor reading.

The American Daffodil Society. *Handbook For Growing, Exhibiting and Judging Daffodils*, 2000. Good source of information for the potential daffodil exhibitor. Our one concern is that some of the cultural information is not accurate. The book was written by amateurs more interested in exhibiting daffodils than in gardening.

Andersen Horticultural Library. *Source List of Plants and Seeds—1999*. List of more than 1,000 cultivars of *Narcissus*, each followed by a source number that can be referenced to material in the front. If you want to know where to find it, try this book.

Blanchard, John. *Narcissus: A Guide to Wild Daffodils*. Alpine Garden Society, 1990. The most complete current work on *Narcissus* in the wild. Written by an expert who has spent many years studying and growing the genus.

Jefferson-Brown, Michael. *Narcissus*. Timber Press, 1991. Written by an Englishman for garden plantings of daffodils in Great Britain, but this book has a good deal of useful information for gardeners everywhere. Brown has spent most of his life growing and selling daffodils. Many of the photographs are of cultivars not commercially available.

The Royal Horticulture Society. *The International Daffodil Register and Classified List*, 1988. A nearly complete listing of every registered daffodil. It contains over 25,000 flower names, color codes, breeders' names, and dates of introduction.

The Royal Horticulture Society. *Yearbook—Daffodils*. Annual booklet of articles primarily about daffodil shows and about growing daffodil and tulip bulbs in Great Britain. Interesting reading for the daffodil addict.

Snazelle, Theodore E. *Daffodil Diseases and Pests*. Middle Tennessee Daffodil Society, 1986. A booklet having all you need to know in order to identify and treat diseases and pests affecting *Narcissus*.

'Holland Sensation' is one of the largest of the bicolor trumpets.

'Camelot' and 'Orange Emperor' both hold up well, last long, and complement each other in companion plantings.

USDA Plant Hardiness Zone Map

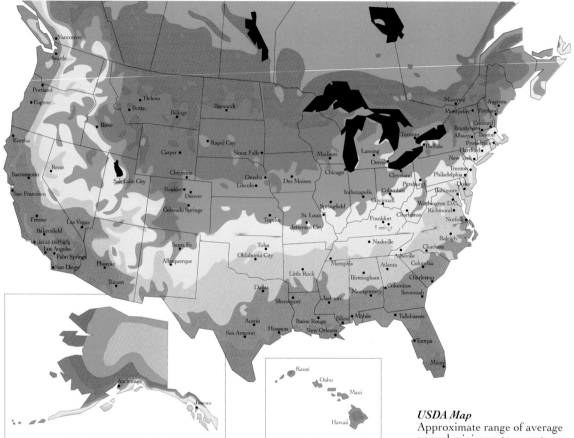

USDA Map
Approximate range of average annual minimum temperatures for each zone.

Zone 1		Below	-50°
Zone 2	-50°	To	-40°
Zone 3	-40°	To	-30°
Zone 4	-30°	To	-20°
Zone 5	-20°	To	-10°
Zone 6	-10°	To	0°
Zone 7	0°	To	10°
Zone 8	10°	To	20°
Zone 9	20°	To	30°
Zone 10	30°	To	40°
Zone 11		Above	40°

There are a number of people that we would like to mention who helped and motivated us to write the first edition of *Daffodils for American Gardens*, and also this updated second edition.

Carolyn Clark, friend, editor, and publisher who was the one who contacted us over and over again and gently pushed until we agreed to write the first edition of *Daffodils*.... and held our hand every pleasurable step of the way.

Frank Robinson, friend, botanist, and horticulturist who checked and corrected some of our botanical terminology.

Mary Lou Gripshover, past Director of the American Daffodil Society and friend who helped us update the ADS Show dates and other daffodil registration information.

Rue Judd of bright sky press, who persuaded us that it was time for the second edition and who made a special trip to help select slides.

Our customers who kept asking for complete gardening information with color pictures.

Index